Jesus, in the Face of His Enemies:

A Paradigm Shift for Overturning Politics as Usual

[In Two Books: The Story, and the Text]

◆ ◆ ◆

John C. Rankin

1

TEI Publishing House
www.teii.org; www.teipublishinghouse.com

The quote from the book of Tobit on pp. 49, 135, is taken from *The New English Bible with the Apocrypha* (Oxford and Cambridge University Presses, 1970).

Cover design by David R. Clarkin.

Preface

This modest book makes some observations about the Passover Week encounters of Jesus en route to the cross. These are central and interpretive realities I have not seen made in church history. The impact can be a unique paradigm shift in the relationship between the Gospel and human politics, if enough Christians grasp and apply what they learn from the biblical text (e.g., my books *Genesis and the Power of True Assumptions*; *The Six Pillars of Biblical Power* and *The Six Pillars of Honest Politics*). And it would be entirely positive for all people of good will.

It is in two parts, or two books, if you will. In Book One, I write it through the plausible first century eyes of the honest Pharisee identified in Mark 12. We name him Baruch (Hebrew for "blessing," a common Jewish name, but not used for any identified New Testament person). An easy read, Book One is written to allow the flow of Baruch's observations to be readily seen, placing us inside the storyline. Thus, biblical quotations, while percolating consistently, are without citation. Any descriptive background is woven into Baruch's experience.

In Book Two, it covers the same territory, but is written descriptively from a 21st century vantage-point, with certain salient background given, and thus all the biblical citations are in place. It is a more proper "study."

We all have our different reading styles, and thus, read the Book that suits you the best. By the same token, this unusual pairing also allows the interested reader, by reading them in succession, to grasp the dynamics more deeply yet. As well, Book One is readily adaptable to a screen play, and that is what inspired it as a complement to the other, which was written first.

Content of Book One: The Story

Chapter One

Why Did Jesus Have Enemies?

Imagine, if we can, seeing Jesus through the eyes of an honest Pharisee. We call him Baruch, and paint a plausible scenario of his encounters with Jesus, hewing closely to the Scriptures while filling in some dialogue that is as consistent as possible. Imagine his line of sight as he personally witnesses the most epic theological and political battle in history – that between Jesus and his sworn enemies. Imagine the decision he has to make when all is said and done.

But too, how is it that Jesus, in healing the sick and raising the dead, has enemies to begin with? Why do the religious and political enemies track his every move once he announces himself? Why does he threaten the status quo? What is the nature of his threat?

Baruch is a rabbi, a teacher of the law, a man in his late-thirties, and well schooled since age four in the Tanakh – the Hebrew Scriptures consisting of the Law, the Prophets and the Writings. He is looking for the Messiah, as is much of the Jewish nation, living under the boot of Roman dominance.

Baruch is a critical thinker, and in fact, so much so that he embraces fully the rabbinic teaching ethic of always posing questions up front in any learning process. He is grateful for this training, but also aware that most of his colleagues are compromised people in this regard – being willing to limit their questions in order to keep social and political position. They are bought off by the Roman authorities, being allowed to maintain their religious stature and economic security because they agree to keep their religion behind the temple and synagogue walls, never to interfere with matters of social justice in the political sphere.

Thus, his relationship with his fellow rabbis is dynamic. On the one hand, they all share much in common in family and social life, and especially, they love to debate theological and historical matters rooted in the Tanakh. On the other hand, he knows, and they know, that he is not a compromised man. He lives within the confines of what Rome expects of the Jewish leadership, but he also holds his distance from agreeing with it. His soul is unsettled as he lives in the tension of being a rabbi who is part of, but not fully part of his rabbinic circle. He is hungry for a freedom he does not yet know how to identify. He looks for the Messiah that is promised one day to come.

Baruch lives in Jerusalem, and like many of his colleagues, hears something of this Jesus, of his quickly growing reputation out of nowhere. This is said to be an uneducated man from the northern country along the Sea of Galilee, next to concentrated Gentile populations. Jesus is called "rabbi" by the common people, and is reputed for healing the sick and driving out demons. He also teaches the people with an authority that is making many of the religious elite jealous. So Baruch makes a trip to the Galilean territory to see for himself.

On a given Sabbath, he runs into six of his colleagues from Jerusalem. He is surprised to see them and quizzical about their purpose – knowing each of them very well – but also experiences a glimmer of hope that they might be reaching for something greater than the status quo.

He joins his well-dressed colleagues as they walk out to the edges of some grainfields of wheat and barley. They approach a man, who along with a dozen other men is picking some heads of grain for a meal.

The lead Pharisee identifies the man named Jesus, and says to him, "Look! Your disciples are doing what is unlawful on the Sabbath." The others joined in the chorus.

Jesus turns to them, looks first at the Pharisaical spokesman, then each of them in turn, and finally, also at Baruch. The clarity of his eyes and authority of speech are immediately compelling, and quintessentially rabbinic.

"Haven't you read what David did when he and his companions were hungry? He entered the house of God, and he and his companions ate the consecrated bread – which was not lawful for them to do, but only for the priests. Or haven't you read in the Law that on the Sabbath the priests in the temple desecrate the day and yet are innocent? I tell you that one greater than

6

the temple is here. If you had known what these words mean, 'I desire mercy, not sacrifice,' you would not have condemned the innocent. For the Son of Man is Lord of the Sabbath."

Baruch's colleagues have no response, standing there as Jesus and his disciples continue to pick heads of grain. They begin to grumble to each other, as they head back toward town: "Who does he think he is? How dare he try to instruct us on the Law?"

Baruch follows a little behind, glancing back a couple of times to the grainfields, and immediately finds himself drawn into the questions posed by Jesus.

Yes, David and his companions did "break" the Law when in a time of need. Yes, the priests do "work" on the Sabbath, and if all work were prohibited on the Sabbath, then it means that their divinely ordained work is really a desecration of the temple, a deeply dangerous sin. This precisely gauged sarcasm, in response, cuts his friends deep, but Baruch probes deeper. For Jesus has merely posed tough questions, rooting himself in shared knowledge of the Tanakh along with the Pharisees. What is the original purpose of the Sabbath?

Then the final "if" question are words quoted from the prophet Hosea – the Lord God desires mercy, not sacrifice. His colleagues are showing no mercy, but also cannot answer Jesus. They live in a ritual cycle of prescribed rules and sacrifices, but all to their own advancement. Jesus and his disciples are taking the prerogative of the poor, as provided for in the Law of Moses – eating from the unharvested edges of the grainfields.

Then the two astounding claims Jesus makes – to be "one" who is greater than the temple, and to declare himself the Son of Man who is Lord of the Sabbath. This is only language that can come from the Messiah, known also as the Son of David, heir to the founding king of Jerusalem.

Baruch's colleagues indeed put their whole identity into the temple, its preservation, and the sacrificial system within its precincts. King Herod the Great had rebuilt it for them in the grandest splendor – with the courtyard still unfinished – some fifty years earlier. It is the Roman bribe to keep the Jewish elite in line. Jesus is a threat to this arrangement, claiming authority over the Pharisees, and in exposing their hypocrisies.

Then, glancing back one more time, Baruch sees Jesus and his disciples also heading toward town, and as soon as his colleagues notice the same, they halt, and recalculate their direction to keep close at his heels. Jesus goes into a local synagogue to teach, and as the Pharisees follow, they see a man standing there with a shriveled hand.

Thus, again, "looking for a reason to accuse Jesus ... they watched him closely to see if he would heal him on the Sabbath."

Jesus looks at the assembly, searching for expectation and hope, and likewise into the eyes of the crippled man. This man, if he were to be identified as a follower of Jesus by the religious authorities, could be expelled from the synagogue. He could be thrown out of his social network that helped provide for his needs, given his handicap in working and providing for himself.

Jesus looks into the eyes of the Pharisaical band, and poses a question. But Baruch now stands off to the side, identifying more as an onlooker than a Pharisee despite his attire.

"Which is lawful on the Sabbath: to do good or to do evil, to save life or to kill?"

Jesus continues to look straight at them, they move their feet nervously as they avert the eye contact, and thus, "they remained silent." The pregnancy of the moment of conflict drapes the room, and indeed, the whole assembly is motionless, breathless, awaiting the words of Jesus.

"He looked around at them in anger and, deeply distressed at their stubborn hearts, said to the man, 'Stretch out your hand.' He stretched it out, and his hand was completely restored. Then the Pharisees went out and began to plot with the Herodians how they might kill Jesus."

Baruch has never seen such intensely heated eyes in a man, of an anger rooted in mercy; and as displayed in the face of those who hated mercy.

Jesus stands in the face of his plotting enemies, and Baruch is captivated by the drama, thinking about nothing else as he returns to Jerusalem.

Later, in a third encounter in observing Jesus, Baruch crosses paths with him in Judea across the Jordan. He observes some of his fellow Pharisees question Jesus on the matter of divorce. In their eyes, feet and body language, Baruch sees unease. They are again engaged in trying to trap Jesus.

And they misrepresent the Torah: "Is it lawful for a man to divorce his wife for any and every reason?" Jesus answers with two crucial passages from creation about marriage as ordained by the Creator, concluding: "So they are no longer two but one. Therefore what God has joined together, let no man separate."

Baruch knows that the very idea of "for any and every reason" has nothing to do with the Law of Moses. Yet, his Pharisaical friends come at it again – "Why did Moses command that a man give his wife a certificate of divorce and send her away?"

Baruch anticipates the answer Jesus gives. Moses "permitted" divorce due to the hardened hearts of men, and the only reason it is ever even permissible is in the case of marital unfaithfulness. But still, not commanded, only permitted as an exception.

Jesus is in control of all he does, and Baruch loves the honest theater.

Chapter Two

The Passover Week Stage

The stage for the drama of the ages begins with the onset of Passover Week.

Baruch continues his work as a teacher of the law for another several years. His obligations and family life keep him in the city. But his experience in having seen Jesus in action is always percolating in the back of his mind and as he continually hears of things Jesus is saying and doing. So often, as he observes his colleagues, as he sees the common people groaning under the weight of the Roman boot, as he studies the Tanakh, he keeps thinking about Jesus, but still has many questions.

Is this the Messiah, or is he yet to come? If he is the Messiah, why does he continue to wander in the northern countryside, yes, showing mercy to the dispossessed, yes, healing the sick and demonized, yes, teaching the Tanakh to the thousands, yes, giving enticing parables that make people think – but when will he come and assume his political authority as the heir to David's throne, and thus drive out the infidel Romans? When will full justice and mercy finally arrive?

It is the first day of Passover Week, and the city is bustling with its regular commerce. But too, the commerce is much greater than normal, as the first of what would proves to be several hundred thousand Jewish pilgrims, including many God-fearing Gentiles, start to arrive. They swell the city some four-fold. Most come on foot, some from nearby, and some come from as far as 1,000 miles. They are there to celebrate the high feast commemorating when the God of Israel led Moses and the twelve tribes out of slavery in Egypt almost 1500 years earlier.

As the Jews pay the annual temple tax in person, they also offer sacrifices in the temple area for their own sins, and they join family and friends for the Passover meal. The Gentile seekers of God observe, and are also be invited to join the Passover celebration, as were pagan Egyptians also invited to join the Israelites in the original pass over by the angel of death just prior to the exodus.

Baruch finds himself outside the Eastern Gate of the city, facing the Mount of Olives. An oncoming commotion draws his attention and he walks in that direction. The city is flooded with stories about Lazarus, a friend of Jesus, having been dead for four days, already wrapped in his grave clothes, already in his burial cave, and then he came back to life at the word of Jesus. The people are following Jesus that much more because of it.

The religious and political elite in the city are nervous. And because of the timing of the Passover Feast, and their incessant monitoring of Jesus, his disciples and their actions and whereabouts, they expect Jesus to show up in Jerusalem. They have already sent some Pharisees to warn Jesus that King Herod wants to kill him. This is self-serving, for their real concern is a coming conflict where they fear Jesus could spark a riot, bring disorder into the city, and cause the Romans to shut down, or even destroy, the temple – their source of identity and income.

The biblical text describes Jesus entering the city:

"As they approached Jerusalem and came to Bethphage on the Mount of Olives, Jesus sent two disciples, saying to them, 'Go to the village ahead of you, and at once you will find a donkey tied there, with her colt by her. Untie them and bring them to me. If anyone says anything to you, tell him that the Lord needs them, and he will send them right away.' "

"This took place to fulfill what was spoken through the prophet:
" 'Say to the Daughter of Zion,
    See, your king comes to you,
gentle and riding on a donkey,
    on a colt, the foal of a donkey.'

"The disciples went and did as Jesus had instructed them. They brought the donkey and the colt, placed their cloaks on them, and Jesus sat on them. A very large crowd spread their cloaks on the road, while others cut branches from the trees and spread them on the road. The crowds that went ahead of him and those that followed shouted,

"Hosanna to the Son of David!"

"Blessed is he who comes in the name of the Lord!"

"Hosanna in the highest!"

"When Jesus entered Jerusalem, the whole city was stirred and asked, 'Who is this?'

"The crowds answered, 'This is Jesus, the prophet from Nazareth in Galilee.' "

There come thousands of people following a man riding a donkey's foal, and Baruch knows it is Jesus, and he rushes to see the procession.

The people understand the language of the Son of David as "the Messiah" in Hebrew ("anointed one"), which in Greek is "the Christ."

When King Herod enters the city, he does so mounted on a prize war stallion, prancing in pride, or perhaps on a chariot, wearing royal garments, with trumpets and a unit of soldiers that shove people out of his way as they lay down a royal carpet, as they announce the "greatness" of the coming "king," and as the people are required to give honor.

In contrast, as Jesus approaches Jerusalem, Baruch sees him riding a young donkey being led by its mother, symbolic of a king who is among the people as a citizen, and not over them as a military conqueror. Baruch knows the Tanakh inside out, and this symbolism immediately leads him to recite to himself the words from the prophet Zechariah: *Say to the Daughter of Zion, See, your king comes to you, gentle and riding on a donkey, on a colt, the foal of a donkey.* What is he witnessing in real time?

These words highlight an unmistakable contrast with worldly political power. Even as Baruch knows that the Messiah will be the ultimate political ruler, he ponders this remarkable symbolism that is consistent with what he knows so far of the character of Jesus.

Jesus rides on the humble cloaks of his disciples, cloaks that are also the carpet of the common people along with the cut palm branches, thrown down in spontaneity. His humility is the opposite of Herod or Caesar's pretense, and the people love it, young and old.

As the people shout and sing their praises, they call out "Hosanna to the Son of David!" "Hosanna" is a term of praise that means "Save!" They also call out "Blessed was he who comes in the name of the Lord!" and "Hosanna in the highest!" Baruch knows the exact location of these words, shouted by the people, from the book of Psalms, and their Messianic nature – just as his mind went immediately to the unspoken words of Zechariah.

The whole city is stirred as Baruch follows Jesus through the Eastern Gate and into the city. He deeply absorbs the intensity of the feelings of all the people. Seven and a half centuries earlier, most of the nation of Israel was carried away into Assyrian captivity, having forsaken the Law of Moses. These Israelites were assimilated into the pagan nations in the subsequent years, including the Samaritans of the first century A.D. The only portion of ancient Israel remaining after the Assyrian conquest was Judah (the Jews) and some others who assimilated into Judah.

Then the Jews lost the city of Jerusalem and the temple 135 years later when *Yahweh Elohim* (Hebrew for the LORD God) allowed their sins to be judged by the Babylonian conquest, destruction and exile. They had forsaken the true worship of Yahweh, with its mercy and justice for all people equally, and alongside the outward form of the temple worship, they worshiped pagan idols, descending into the practices of sorcery, sacred prostitution and child sacrifice. This is a contradiction in terms, where they could not outwardly deny Yahweh, while inwardly lusting for gods they thought they could somehow control.

The temple had been rebuilt in modesty since, at Yahweh's directive, prior to Herod the Great rebuilding it. But apart from a period of independence, the

Jews were otherwise occupied by various foreign powers that did not regard Yahweh as the true God.

Baruch's fellow Jews yearn for freedom, and here is Jesus – with authority, miracles and words of comfort. He comes into the city, being proclaimed the Son of David.

Chapter Three

Contest Engaged

Baruch knows well the threat Jesus is posing to his colleagues and the Roman Empire at the same time. The majority of the religious elite are compromised people, as Rome is adroit in its treatment of the conquered Jews. It does not seek to wipe out their leadership per se. Rather it seeks to bring them into the Roman political order, and give them the temple as a vested interest, so as not to rebel against Rome if external or internal threats ever arise.

The Jewish people are also a great thorn in Rome's side, not bowing down to her pagan assumptions, to an admixture of polytheism and the imperial cult of Caesar, as do other subjects. They passionately resist Roman rule (sometimes in bloody clashes), and likewise have gained exemption from military conscription – the only people conquered by Rome able to do so.

The original temple of the Israelites was built by King Solomon nearly 1,000 years earlier, but it and the city were destroyed some 400 years later by the Babylonians. Baruch knows the warnings given by God to Solomon, and then through the prophets, not to make an idol of the temple as do pagan nations with their temples. But the Judahite remnant ended up doing so, and judgment came.

As Baruch considers this reality, and sees Jesus, he also sees more clearly how most of the religious elite are now treating the temple as an idol once again. They fear its loss so deeply, and so fear any attempt to bring social justice into the political order, that they are consistently plotting to kill Jesus.

After his entry, Jesus goes straight toward the temple.

"Jesus entered the temple area and drove out all who were buying and selling there. He overturned the tables of the money changers and the benches of those selling doves. 'It is written,' he said to them, 'My house will be called a house of prayer,' but you are making it a 'den of robbers.' "

Baruch follows Jesus into the Court of the Gentiles, a large walled area surrounding the temple where Gentiles are welcome to seek and learn of the God of Israel, the one true Creator, without first having to undergo circumcision and other requirements to become Jewish.

As the Jewish pilgrims come to offer their sacrifices and pay the temple tax, they are greeted in the courtyard by fellow Jews, businessmen. First they see the money changers, who change their foreign coin into Tyrian coin, the local currency required to pay the temple tax.

And second, they see those selling the animals required for sacrifice, from the doves or pigeons for the poor, to the heifers or goats for the wealthy. Most of the business is for the poor who have traveled significant distances, being unable to bring their sacrifices with them.

Baruch knows this is a legitimate business need, but too, it should be done outside the temple courts, and for a fair price. As well, these entrepreneurs also know that by doing business in the temple courts, they can command a higher, indeed, a usurious rate. It is a matter of convenience inside an aura of religious practice. And just as he had seen the anger of Jesus against his colleagues those years earlier in the Galilean synagogue, Baruch now sees it again. Jesus is furious with hypocrites who preyed on the needy.

Baruch looks at the money changers and those selling sacrificial animals. They are terrified at what is happening, knowing they are about to suffer great financial loss, perhaps their largest portion of income for the year. But too, they are Jews, knowing that they are ripping off fellow Jews in the name of religion, and their consciences are rattled by the words of Jesus. They also fear that if Jesus were to anger the Romans too much, Herod would send in a cohort of soldiers and shut down Passover week altogether.

Baruch sees this "gentle king" Jesus coming, with thousands following him, straight to their place of business. The noise grows as a wave of humanity approach behind him. There are already thousands of people in the courtyard to begin with, including those lined up to pay their temple tax or purchase their doves or larger animals, and those performing their sacrifices across the courtyard at the times of evening and morning sacrifice. This "gentle king" is not so gentle with the "den of robbers."

The benches of those selling doves are just inside each of the ten gates, several to one side; and to the other side, several tables of the money changers. Jesus makes a whip of cords on the spot, and like herding animals he snaps it while driving the merchants away, "Get these out of here!" The merchants make a quick and desperate calculation, for this is the worst of two possibilities.

First, they are being ordered to close down business as the Romans might do if they were to shut down Passover week altogether. But the Romans might also have allowed them to take their doves and animals with them, and gather their sacks of various coins before leaving. And second, they are being chastised by Jesus, who quotes a Messianic prophecy. He is angry, their consciences are pricked, and they have no time to collect their possessions.

They are forced to flee, but no further away than they can manage, always looking back at what is happening to their possessions. If they are selling birds or livestock, they have to watch their benches overturned one after the other, landing hard against the stone pavement. The caged birds or penned animals are agitated, and commotion ensues. On top of this, Jesus halts all related business in this de facto bazaar.

And too, the money changers watch from a safe distance as Jesus approaches their forcibly abandoned tables. Behind them are many sacks of coin from various nations in the Diaspora from which so many Jews have traveled. They and their colleagues do business with many tens of thousands of households, and their tables have neat piles of gold, silver, copper and other coins.

Jesus extends his arms and hands from his robe, sweeping the piles of coin onto the uneven pavement, and they roll as far as the pavement allows. The common people see this money from where they stand, and can easily imagine how one gold coin could be worth half a year's wages. Then the money changers see Jesus grasp the rear corner and front leg of a table, still with some coins on it, to lift the back forward and as it lands hard on the stone pavement.

Jesus now has the complete attention of the large crowd, and declares "It is written ..." With these opening words, the whole crowd quiets immediately, even the displaced merchants. The Jews know well the Hebrew Scriptures from childhood. Baruch does even more so, like his fellow rabbis. And the Gentiles present, being seekers of the God of Israel as the true God, are also oftentimes well versed in the Hebrew Bible. Too, the people are looking for the Messiah, and they have heard or are among those who had shouted Messianic prophecies moments earlier. They all know that when these words are stated, the written Word of God is about to be quoted.

"My house will be called ..." The people are poised for a Messianic prophecy to be fulfilled, and as soon as these quoted words are uttered, the majority of them know what words are to follow. They know exactly where in the scrolls of Isaiah and Jeremiah these words are found.

Also, in this singular moment, the people are enthralled with Jesus, for he is speaking with great authority, "My house," spoken by the owner.

For the common people, this is good news. But for the religious elitists, this is blasphemy – or they were rationalizing the same in their opposition to Jesus. The common people are overjoyed, the elitists infuriated. And all those within hearing range are listening closely as Jesus speaks. The house of prayer for all nations is being prostituted into a "den of robbers," and Jesus, acting as the Messiah, has come to pronounce judgment on this state of affairs.

Baruch continues to ponder. And one point he considers why no one challenges Jesus when he halts the business activity in the temple courts. The merchants do not try to protest – they know they are guilty. The religious elitists do not protest – the people believe they are guilty at a deeper level, prostituting their teaching and leadership offices for their own power, prostituting the temple in service to Rome. The common people are watching and loving this true and dynamic theater. Baruch watches the theater too, looking at Jesus, looking at the merchants, looking at his colleagues, thinking it through. *The man who has just been hailed as the coming Messiah is behaving like the Messiah – cleansing the house of God as his first act in entering the city.*

Contest engaged.

Chapter Four

Falling Into Their Own Trap

As the dishonest merchants scramble, as the people accordingly have joy, Jesus turns and heads to the temple itself. The crowds follow him, and the religious elitists are determined to keep up with him. Baruch too joins the throng, as his head is exploding with a thousand elements of the Tanakh he knows and loves so well, wondering what Jesus will do next.

"The blind and the lame came to him at the temple, and he healed them. But when the chief priests and the teachers of the law saw the wonderful things he did and the children shouting in the temple area, 'Hosanna to the Son of David,' they were indignant.

" 'Do you hear what these children are saying?' they asked him.

" 'Yes,' replied Jesus, 'have you never read, "From the lips of children and infants you have ordained praise"?'

"And he left them and went out of the city to Bethany, where he spent the night."

Baruch remembers the question posed by Jesus in the grainfields concerning mercy. Here, as he sees Jesus execute judgment on the usurious merchants, mercy is what follows. Judgment and mercy are two commanding themes in the Tanakh, where mercy is not possible unless judgment is first acknowledged. And here is Jesus, in his actions thus far seen by Baruch, and according to his wider reputation, being consistent. Baruch sees that those who hate mercy hate Jesus, and those who seek mercy flock to Jesus.

Baruch understands that according to his rabbinic training, the blind and the lame are "unclean," and not to be allowed access to the "holy" temple. Yet here they are in its very shadow, coming to Jesus to be healed, and the enemies of Jesus do not protest. Then too, how can they? These healings are done in their presence, the facts cannot be denied, and they remember their inability to answer Jesus in the grainfields and the synagogue. It is not the

20

Sabbath, so this excuse for opposition has already been silenced, and they lack the courage to make another excuse based on their interpretation of Scripture.

As the Pharisaical band watches, a separate group of their colleagues approach – the chief priests, the epitome of Jewish religious authority, along with some fellow teachers of the law. They too witness the healings, and then their anger is especially aroused when the little children shout and sing "Hosanna to the Son of David."

Baruch notes that this is their point of indignation. For Jesus to be proclaimed the Son of David, means that he is the heir of the founding king of Jerusalem. This is a baldly political claim, Jesus does not refute it when he approaches the city to the throngs who proclaim it, and now he is not refusing the children who say the same.

Though Baruch cannot yet put the pieces together as to why Jesus has yet to make any political move, he wonders if it is now pending. He understands the reaction of the chief priests and their cohort, for they fear greatly that such a claim can spark the riot they have long feared, and thus lose the temple and their power.

The chief priests and teachers of the law are exercised inside themselves by the presence of the blind and the lame. And yet before they can fully process it, they see these little barefooted urchins, the children of the uneducated common people, calling for the stuff of political rebellion in naming the Son of David. These children have witnessed their parents calling Jesus the Son of David. Now that they witness the authority of Jesus in the face of hypocrisy, along with his power to heal the blind and the lame, they repeat with enthusiasm what their parents have taught them. Jesus is behaving just like the Messiah is supposed to behave.

Baruch has heard talk among some of his colleagues, including the group of Pharisees who went to warn Jesus a few days earlier about Herod. He also has heard how the Sanhedrin has met on how to deal with "the Jesus problem."

The Sanhedrin is the ruling council of the Jews permitted by the Romans to rule in religious matters. Here, their various members want to find some pretext to arrest Jesus out of sight of the people. But apparently, Jesus has thus far evaded them, and too, the people are always following him.

Baruch watches the chief priests pose a question, not for the purpose of learning – as all the onlookers can easily discern – but in an attempt to silence Jesus. They have studied the Tanakh supremely, they know it in Hebrew, Aramaic and Greek, forward and backward, and can identify every jot and tittle from every conceivable angle. They are furious that Jesus is allowing these despised and obviously ignorant children to quote the Scripture in such a way.

They are seeking to trap Jesus in his words, and quite ineptly as Baruch thinks about it. In fact, it appears as though Jesus walks into this and their other traps quite deliberately. Baruch is grasping their increased desperation as they ask Jesus if he hears what the children are saying.

Now, clearly, Jesus "hears." So there is a deeper agenda at play, where the chief priests are trying to play to their own strengths. As well, Jesus is reputed to have healed many deaf people, something to which the chief priests and their allies cannot lay claim.

No, they know Jesus hears the children. They are indignant, sarcastic and insulting – their anger is dripping in the face of this man. It is time to cut Jesus down to size. They are saying Jesus does not "understand," that he is a pretender, and they are about to prove it. They want Jesus to trip over his own words, for if it happens but once, they can justify themselves in their opposition to him – both inwardly and in public.

This contest further sets Baruch's mind spinning. Their sarcasm occasions him to think that they are trying to fashion themselves after the prophet Elijah. This Hebrew prophet once confronted 450 prophets of the Canaanite deity Ba'al, along with 400 prophets of Asherah (Ba'al's female consort), in a contest on Mount Carmel. These pagan prophets served King Ahab, and his Sidonian wife and witch, Queen Jezebel, who was murdering as many Hebrew prophets as she could. The contest was designed to place Yahweh

22

and Ba'al side by side in competing sacrifices and prayers. It was one prophet in the face of 850, to see whether Ba'al or Yahweh would answer with fire from heaven, and thus be proven as the living God.

In the process, the 450 prophets of Ba'al called on their god from morning to noon, also later resorting to self-inflicted bloodletting, and as no answer came, Elijah taunted them. He said that their god either could not hear them, was lost in thought, relieving himself, or traveling.

Baruch sees this as the nature of the sarcasm employed against Jesus by the chief priests. They are saying that Jesus is a false prophet, in service to a pagan god like Ba'al who cannot "hear," that he is no Messiah. They assume their superiority in handling the Scripture, and this implicit reference to Elijah is meant to demonstrate their dexterity in argument.

Too, the chief priests and teachers of the law are using this tactic to achieve something even more important – get Jesus to shut the children up, and prevent a collision with Rome.

It is obvious to Baruch and the crowd that Jesus is unfazed by this bravado. Jesus answers "Yes," and a smile brightens his face. Baruch is surprised, but then as he processes it quickly, is unsurprised. It is a smile of a man who is confident, humble and at peace with himself. Jesus, in looking at his enemies face to face, both loves them and necessarily opposes their hypocrisies. Their mouths are pursed, their eyes pained, their postures ill at ease and their fists tightening.

The more Baruch sees Jesus in action, the more he appreciates how so many people, friend and foe of Jesus alike, have spoken to him about the words and actions of Jesus being "amazing." Baruch is amazed as he sees this conflict unfold, his amazement has been growing the whole time, and he now begins to sense he has seen only a little of what he will see.

So Jesus continues, with a cheerful but focused expression, posing his question in response, "Have you never read ...?" A reversal, yet ratcheting up, of the sarcasm and insults his enemies threw his way.

The chief priests and teachers of the law now burn with greater anger. Jesus is turning the tables on them, showing his dexterity, and Baruch sees that Jesus is the more skillful rabbi. He is about to pose a question concerning their competency in reading the Scriptures, in response to a dishonest question of entrapping intent. Here, in this moment, in the middle of Jesus' sentence, Baruch clearly sees that the chief priests are about to fall into their own trap.

They know Jesus hears what the children are saying, and Jesus knows how well his enemies have read the Tanakh. Baruch sees their pride explode in the face of this uneducated pretender from the northern country by the Gentiles.

They know they can neither contest the teachings of Jesus, nor how the common people respect his authority. As well, they certainly cannot challenge the reality of his many miracles. But Jesus is probing deeper to see if they understand the text. He asks them if they have read a clause from the eighth psalm: " 'From the lips of children and infants you have ordained praise ...' "

Jesus, speaking in Aramaic, quotes from the Septuagint, the Greek translation of the Hebrew Bible. It was done by a group of some seventy Jewish scholars several centuries earlier, when Jewish exiles were spread throughout the Greek world, where in their synagogues the vernacular of the culture was necessary. It was translated over a period of 38 years, with excruciating faithfulness in how to render the text from Hebrew to Greek. Baruch sees how Jesus is being precise in his translation reference.

But especially, Jesus does something shrewd and powerful – he stops the quote in the middle of the original grammatical sentence, focusing on the positive elements of the children's praise in giving answer. The chief priests and teachers of the law know he is stopping the sentence mid-stream. Jesus leaves them to fill in the rest.

When Jesus earlier quoted Isaiah and Jeremiah, "It is written ..." and "My house ...," he knew most if not all of the onlookers knew what words were to follow. They knew the Messianic texts, and were placing their hope in them.

Even more so, the chief priests and teachers of the law know the Tanakh by heart, and as Jesus stops in the middle of the sentence, what do they do? They automatically continue, in their minds, with the rest of that sentence of the Messianic prophecy, if not more. Jesus deliberately causes this to happen, and as Baruch watches on, he knows the words from the eighth psalm that follow: "… because of your enemies, to silence the foe and the avenger."

Baruch senses a defining moment at hand as Jesus, eyeball-to-eyeball with his enemies, is in control of the language. He knows that the word translated in the Greek as "praise" comes from the Hebrew text of the Tanakh, from the root word for "strength." And he knows the history of Nehemiah, the Jewish governor of Jerusalem after the Babylonian exile. As he oversaw the rebuilding of the city walls in the face of strong opposition from Judah's enemies, and in giving comfort to the people, Nehemiah declared "… the joy of the LORD is your strength."

In other words, a deliberate play on words sets up what is to follow.

Baruch knows that the "strength" of children is represented in their "praise" of, their hosannas to Jesus as the Son of David. Baruch knows that the word for "infants" refers to newborn children at their mother's breasts – those whose babblings are both praise and strength. Baruch knows that his fellow rabbis know all this too.

Baruch knows that in the Tanakh all judgment from the Lord comes solely in concert with people's self-chosen deeds and words. Thus, now, the chief priests, et al., stand on this very precipice. They know that the unspoken words in the balance of the sentence from the eighth psalm equal their self-condemnation unless they publicly distance themselves from it – "because of your enemies, to silence the foe and the avenger."

But how can they do so, given the depth of their hatred and the hole they have dug for themselves? Their pride leads the way. If they dare to challenge Jesus further here, and too, if they do anything less than agree with Jesus, they remain stuck. Their self-righteous anger burns more deeply yet, but they are impotent to speak it without exposing themselves. They are on the verge of an unspoken, sub-textual but publicly understood confession that they are the enemies of the Messiah. Jesus allows all this to understatedly manifest, as the crowd and Baruch watch with amazement.

Baruch also knows that the frustration of the chief priests and teachers of the law is rooted in a deeper agenda that is failing to work out as hoped. They are in essence telling Jesus to shut up the children's praise, and to stop all this political talk about him being the Son of David. In response, Jesus gives an unmistakable message, as if to say: "Not only will I not shut them up, but their praise, which you despise, is my strength. You are the foes of the Messiah, I am the Messiah and their praise will silence you instead. Any further questions gentlemen?"

Explosive.

Baruch also knows that there is another sub-textual element that ratchets up the challenge. The chief priests want to disprove Jesus as the Messiah, to show him failing to fulfill the messianic prophecies thus far quoted. If they can find but one point where they can rationalize a failure on his part, they can win the debate in their minds. They are still searching for the one point.

Jesus knows this, so he makes another sub-textual challenge, in the spirit of precise sarcasm, as if to say: "Gentlemen, all you have to do to prove that I am not the Messiah is to keep on babbling like babies, to keep on talking. For, if you are able, you can disprove the eighth psalm and show that you are not the enemies of the true Messiah." But, ironically, if they babble like infants, they embrace the "weakness" they despise. They have only created a trap for themselves that Jesus now identifies.

As well, Baruch considers his earlier thoughts about the chief priests seeking to implicitly identify themselves with Elijah versus the pagan prophets of Ba'al, seeking to put Jesus into the category of a deaf god, a false messiah. Baruch now knows that Jesus is aware of this ploy, for he gives it back to them, likewise with implicit reference.

Namely, the language of the eighth psalm, in referring to "infants," is a reference to children at their mother's breasts, so young that they cannot speak articulately, but only babble. The children who shout "Hosanna to the

26

Son of David" are older and articulate, yet they are regarded by the chief priests as weak and despised. So Jesus, in quoting the eighth psalm, takes some "babbling" children, weaker and more despised yet by the elitists, and employs their faith and innocence as an example of his strength in the face of their pretense. Jesus allows the Messianic language of the strength and power of the coming king to merge with the essence of humility found in the youngest of children.

Baruch knows that the word "babble" traces back to the Tower of Babel, in its confusion of languages and nations. He knows that Jesus is hinting at a double entendre – babbling is the strength of little children, but weakness and folly for adults. "Babbling" adults trace back to the original source of paganism and polity that challenged Yahweh Elohim, back to Babylonian religion, back to the peoples who destroyed Solomon's temple and city of Jerusalem some 600 years earlier. Jesus is thus hinting: "Who and what, gentlemen, are truly pagan?"

Then, to conclude, Jesus essentially lays down the gauntlet, declaring that if his enemies do not silence themselves, they will triumph.

What a simple offer, and yet the nuances are many, for all they have to do is babble like a newborn or toddler – they do not have to be cogent or truthful, they just have to resist being silenced by the strength of childlikeness. Baruch can see both the shrewdness and innocence in the wisdom of Jesus. His enemies now bristle at such an analogy, given their mockery of the children. They had sought to dig a pit for Jesus, but they themselves fall into it.

Essentially, Jesus gives them an offer they cannot refuse – an invitation to rake him over the coals with their toughest ad hoc questions, to an honest debate on the most gracious terms possible. Jesus will be teaching in the Court of the Gentiles during Passover week to the throngs, they are invited to attend, and they only have to maintain the power of a filibuster to disprove Jesus as the Messiah.

The debate is set.

Their chosen descent into the hell of their own trap is gathering force.

They were free to step out of their trap anytime, but it appeared that they loved their idols of the temple and political power more than truth and mercy.

Chapter Five

The Question of Authority

The eyeball-to-eyeball intensity between Jesus and his enemies is remarkable for Baruch and the onlookers to witness – especially for the blind who have just been healed. His authority is unmatched, and it is good news for all who are seeking release from the idolatrous arrangement between the religious elitists and the occupying Roman Empire. They are watching Jesus accept the mantle of the Son of David, they see his actions as the Messiah, and they can judge the soul of Jesus, out of whom the light shines, versus the souls of the religious elitists, into whom the darkness retreats.

Baruch continues to process it all. As the chief priests and the teachers of the law challenge Jesus, he sees that they do not challenge him on the facts of the case. They do not challenge his reason to overturn the tables of the money changers, or the benches of those selling doves, or the rightness of it, and they do not challenge his healings as fake or inappropriate.

But they bristle at the language of the Son of David, and need to find some way to discredit Jesus. To do so, they have to move away from the question of the Son of David, and find some other route, some secondary questions.

So the first day of the week moves toward its end. The chief priests and the Pharisees walk away from the temple, while Jesus continues to heal the sick, drive out demons, and begins to teach the people.

Baruch now does something bold. His colleagues know he is not a compromised man, but he has also worked within the system to this point. In his conversations with them, he hews closely to good rabbinic questions, and given his skill, always keeps his colleagues in a place of respect, if also with some tension. They themselves have had many separate and impassioned intramural debates concerning Jesus and his nature. They know Baruch is carefully considering Jesus, and that he is in fact taken with Jesus. But they cannot find fault with him, and besides which, it is Jesus whom they fear and concentrate their energies on.

As Jesus is fully occupied with the people, and as Baruch is not yet ready to speak with him directly, he approaches some of his disciples. He begins to ask them questions, but also holds a certain distance, diplomatically walking a fine line in such a charged atmosphere. After awhile, Jesus and his disciples leave the temple area, and Baruch heads home. When he arises in the morning, he says his prayers, washes, eats, and heads to the temple area.

As he does, he sees Jesus and his disciples already there. Jesus is teaching a large crowd of people, and more are streaming in his direction all the time. While making his way through the crowd, Baruch runs into two of the disciples with whom he had conversed the prior day.

They are in a discussion with each other, and are happy to include Baruch. They share with him how they and Jesus spent the night outside the city, in the neighboring town of Bethany. Earlier that morning, as they walked back to the city, they watched Jesus look for some figs on a fig tree, but there were none, though it was in full bloom. So Jesus cursed the tree, and it withered.

What did this mean? They discussed the matter, about how this tree was strange, having leaves but producing no fruit. They also discussed how the fig tree was a symbol for the nation of Israel in the Tanakh, and if the curse given by Jesus had any deeper meaning.

The biblical text:

"When the disciples saw this, they were amazed. "How did the fig tree wither so quickly?" they asked.

"Jesus replied, 'I tell you the truth, if you have faith and do not doubt, not only can you do what was done to the fig tree, but you can also say to this mountain, "Go, and throw yourself into the sea," and it will be done. If you believe, you will receive whatever you ask for in prayer.' "

When Jesus speaks these words, he and the disciples have in view the whole city, with the imposing temple atop Mount Zion, a descriptive name for Jerusalem as the City of David.

Looking also at Mount Zion, and thinking too of the cursed fig tree, Baruch says to himself a clause from the second psalm: *I have installed my King on Zion, my holy hill.* Another tantalizing question now arises in his mind concerning Jesus and the political mission of the Messiah. Jesus is always touching on its very edges, yet also keeping his distance.

Baruch now wanders in his mind to some words of Isaiah: *Of the increase of his government and peace there will be no end. He will reign on David's throne and over his kingdom, establishing it and upholding it with justice and righteousness from that time on and forever. The zeal of the LORD Almighty will accomplish this.*

Baruch has seen the zeal of Jesus with the money changers and those selling doves. Now, is Jesus actually cursing Mount Zion where the Messiah is supposed to reign? Or is he giving spiritual authority for his disciples to remove the idolatry of the temple and Roman government, predicting the overthrow of both? Will then the Messiah take political authority? Or is Baruch missing something more?

Now that Jesus has come back to the Court of the Gentiles, Baruch also notices that the same religious elite, with more of their colleagues, are also standing at the edge of the crowd closest to Jesus.

The biblical text continues:

"Jesus entered the temple courts, and, while he was teaching, the chief priests and the elders of the people came to him. 'By what authority are you doing these things?' they asked. 'And who gave you this authority?'

"Jesus replied, 'I will also ask you one question. If you answer me, I will tell you by what authority I am doing these things. John's baptism – where did it come from? Was it from heaven, or from men?'

"They discussed it among themselves and said, 'If we say, "From heaven," he will ask, "Then why didn't you believe him?" But if we say, "From men" – we are afraid of the people, for they all hold that John was a prophet.'

31

"So they answered Jesus, 'We don't know.'

"Then he said, 'Neither will I tell you by what authority I am doing these things.' "

Again, Baruch is amazed at this next round in the debate, and the aplomb and rabbinic excellence by which Jesus handles himself. The chief priests have brought along some of the elders of the people in a new attempt to silence Jesus. They use their trump card – Jesus is not from Jerusalem, he has not studied in one of the city's rabbinic schools – he has not sat at the feet of a rabbi to study the Tanakh. Thus, he has no official "authority" or credentials to teach and heal, and thus, no one should listen to him.

Jesus meets them head on. He respects their training, and since the chief priests are given their religious authority by means of an elite education, Jesus challenges them to live up to the ability of true elites. He welcomes their freedom to rake him over the coals with their best questions.

As if to say, thought Baruch: *If you ask me a leading question, fine. But first show me the integrity of answering my leading question, and then I will know if you are truly elite, able to take in what you dish out.*

Thousands of people are listening to Jesus. In response to his question, the chief priests and elders huddle in the midst of the crowd, with all the people watching, with those close enough seeking to listen in. Baruch also makes sure he has a clear earshot to the discussion. His colleagues look nervous, an island of insecurity in the midst of a people they have the pretense enough to think they rule.

As they discuss it among themselves, they quickly boil it down to two options.

First is to admit the truth as the people believe it, but for which they cannot dare admit – that John the Baptist received his authority from heaven.

Baruch knows all the religious leaders in Jerusalem, having had many conversations in their midst, and having overheard many others. Here he sees some Pharisees who had told him about visiting John the Baptist at the River Jordan several years earlier, having been sent by their colleagues to see who he was, and what he was up to. They came back furious, as John rebuked them for hypocrisy. It stung, and they complained about it for some time.

These Pharisees, along with their colleagues, could not contest John's authority, and as they could not find in him any deviation from the Tanakh. So here in this circle, the chief priests and the elders are not going to revisit this debate in the presence of Jesus, and they are not going to acknowledge that John the Baptist had any true authority. They know that John testified to Jesus as the Messiah, and to accept John's authority as heavenly meant they now have to also believe in Jesus – the one thing they are firmly in opposition to doing.

The second option is no more palatable – to seek to market a lie as the people would regard it, saying that John the Baptist received his authority from human imagination.

Baruch watches. During the discussion, the elders look nervously over their shoulders at all the people, clearly fearing them and not wanting to arouse their opposition. They speak candidly with each other, fearing that if they say that John only had human authority, the people will stone them to death on the spot. The people hung on the words of John, they hang on the words of Jesus, and the chief priests and elders of the people know it well.

They are trapped again, having sought to trap Jesus again. They have to choose a third option – the pretension of ignorance, the "we don't know" argument. It is the only way out of their dilemma if they want to keep alive and keep their positions intact.

Baruch's amazement is unceasing – he sees the chief priests, the highest "authorities" among the Jews fall flat on their faces as they try to assert their authority over Jesus, in mocking his "authority." Now, more striking yet, along with the elders: *Are they reduced to the point of pretending not to know something?*

Baruch knows that as they do so, they are also consciously reducing themselves to the status of Cain – the forefather of the lineage that led to those who opposed the Messianic and Davidic line. The Son of David theme, which they are seeking to avoid in this new round of the debate, still manages to percolate. But since they are not going to grant or deny John the acknowledgement of divine authority, what else can they do? Baruch can see the pain of their inner turmoil, etched on their faces writ large. They condescend to no possible alternative but an admission of ignorance in the presence of this non-credentialed Jesus.

Cain murdered his brother Abel out of jealously. His afterthought offering to Yahweh had been rejected, while Abel's conscientious offering of his best had been accepted. Yahweh offered Cain the freedom to change, but Cain looked away from Yahweh instead. His hatred of God thus led to his hatred and murder of his brother.

As Abel's blood cried "from the ground," Yahweh quizzed Cain, "Where is your brother?" Cain answered, "I don't know … Am I my brother's keeper?" Cain would not admit the truth that he had killed Abel, for then he would have to repent. And he could not market the lie that Abel was indeed alive, only somewhere else. He knew he could not fool the Lord. So he pretended to be ignorant.

This is exactly the pattern now repeating itself in the face of Jesus. Baruch glances at one of the chief priests whom he knows well, and in his eyes he sees the acknowledgement of this reality. But also this chief priest is upset with Baruch, for he knows he is of a different mind.

Baruch sees the respect by which Jesus treats his enemies, but too, since they refuse to rise to the ethics of classic rabbinic debate, Jesus does not demean them by answering their question. He is calling them to a higher standard than they expect of themselves, he is calling them to be who they should be in their leadership roles.

Jesus again defines the terms of the debate. His enemies continue to stand there with nothing more to say and Jesus continues his response by saying "What do you think?" From here he gives three parables. The first parable concerns two sons – one who promises obedience then reneges, and the other, who disobeys but later changes his mind and obeys.

The second parable concerns tenants who rebel against their master and eventually kill the master's son in an attempt to steal the land. The third parable concerns a wedding banquet where the invited guests refuse the invitation, and the king thus invites the poor and needy to take their places.

In each parable Jesus profiles those who will inherit God's kingdom, and those who will not. In each case it is people such as tax collectors (i.e., "traitors" since they are in the employ of Rome) and prostitutes who repent, and not the elitists who view it as their privileged domain and "right." In the second parable, Jesus challenges his enemies the way he does in first by turning the tables on them:

"Jesus said to them, 'Have you never read in the Scriptures:

'The stone the builders rejected
   has become the capstone;
the Lord has done this,
   and it is marvelous in our eyes'?

" 'Therefore I tell you that the kingdom of God will be taken away from you and given to a people who will produce its fruit. He who falls on this stone will be broken to pieces, but he on whom it falls will be crushed.'

"When the chief priests and the Pharisees heard Jesus' parables, they knew he was talking about them. They looked for a way to arrest him, but they were afraid of the crowd because the people held that he was a prophet."

In the first parable, Baruch knows that the chief priests and the Pharisees understand that they are being likened to the second son who said he would obey his father, but did not. But the "tax collectors and the prostitutes are entering the kingdom of God ahead of you," for they are like the first son who initially disobeyed his father, then changed his mind and obeyed.

In the second parable, Jesus identifies his enemies as the killers of the vineyard owner's son, and then quotes a Messianic psalm showing them to be those who reject the "capstone," the Messiah. Jesus knows they are plotting to kill him, they know he knows, and now Jesus puts in their face a parable that diagnoses this reality. They have a choice, but remained silent.

Jesus is in full control. The religious elitists, being well educated and proud, are nonetheless silenced in the presence of this so-called pretender. They refuse to engage him in honest debate. In the wake of the first two parables, they do not engage Jesus, but they again huddle among themselves, surrounded by a crowd of people they fear. Jesus continues with his third parable concerning the wedding banquet, where the same themes are reiterated – their rejection of the kingdom of God, and the acceptance by the needy.

The encounter with the eighth psalm the day before leads the chief priests and elders to challenge the authority and credentials of Jesus. It too fails, and they are again silenced. Baruch's wonder grows.

Chapter Six

Paying Taxes to Caesar

Another attempt comes the next day, with Jesus again teaching at the temple to the crowds, and Baruch again being present.

"Then the Pharisees went out and laid plans to trap him in his words. They sent their disciples to him along with the Herodians. 'Teacher,' they said, 'we know you are a man of integrity and that you teach the way of God in accordance with the truth. You aren't swayed by men, because you pay no attention to who they are. Tell us then, what is your opinion? Is it right to pay taxes to Caesar or not?'

"But Jesus, knowing their evil intent, said, 'You hypocrites, why are you trying to trap me? Show me the coin used for paying the tax.' They brought him a denarius, and he asked them, 'Whose portrait is this? And whose inscription?'

" 'Caesar's,' they replied. Then he said to them, 'Give to Caesar what is Caesar's, and to God what is God's.'

"When they heard this, they were amazed. So they left him and went away."

Silenced, again.

Baruch is a Pharisee, and he knows well the make-up of his sect. They are theologically orthodox, they are nationalists who oppose the Roman occupation, and some of them are calculating agitators waiting for the right moment to see the Roman yoke cast off. Part of that calculation is their toleration of working with Rome and Herod in the meantime, insofar as necessary. Baruch too is theologically orthodox, believing in the Tanakh as the written Word of God, and all teachings thus derived. He is also a nationalist, is looking for freedom from the Roman boot, and accordingly, looking for the Messiah. But he is not comfortable in a system governed by the compromise of Rome and the temple. He is not of one mind with his fellow Pharisees who seem to make the Messianic hope secondary to their nationalism.

Baruch, too, knows well the Herodians, and does not trust them for an inch. They are an eclectic and opportunistic lot, and they support the rule of the Herods (being an Edomite, from Esau's line) in preference to direct rule by Roman prefects. Some are Sadducees, who make up the majority of the Sanhedrin, and are the wealthiest of the religious elite. They are also theologically heterodox, deeply opposed by the Pharisees on theological terms. The Herodians hold together by political opinions, not theological ones. They oppose and are opposed by the Pharisees. Mixed up and at cross-purposes in many directions.

But though the Pharisees and Herodians hate each other, they hate Jesus more. So they conspire against him. This is a classic example of a common proverb in Baruch's world: "The enemy of my enemy is my friend." But too, as Baruch knows, at least until the mutual enemy is destroyed, after which newfound friends return to their old ways and become each other's enemies once again.

They have a mutual fear of Jesus, whom they perceive as a threat to both of their elitist positions. Thus, some disciples of the Pharisees, along with the Herodians, put aside their mutual distrust for the moment and conspire to entrap Jesus.

These momentary allies figure they can get him from both sides at once. From the Pharisaical perspective, the question of credentials did not work, so now they devise a plan to trap him in the crosshairs of political versus religious authority.

They send some of their disciples along with the hated Herodians. This reveals their insecurity, for having already been directly silenced, the Pharisees now shield their egos with proxies.

These Pharisaical disciples begin with flattery. They know, and Jesus knows that they know, as Baruch knows, and as the people in the Court of the Gentiles know, this is an inept attempt for the sake of an ulterior agenda.

Yet when the best argument they can make is a "We don't know" posture, the moral ineptitude is clear as it only gathers speed in its downward spiral. Their spokesman clears his throat and attempts to sound sincere, knowing the whole while his ruse.

Baruch quickly notes the phoniness. The Pharisees have already tried to silence Jesus as a man without true authority, yet now in their desperation, their disciples pretend to honor him as one with such authority.

What the Pharisees would not admit, their disciples now pretend to admit: "You aren't swayed by men, because you pay no attention to who they are." In other words, they de facto admit that truth tellers are not impressed or influenced by social elitists. And at the same time they are frustrated with Jesus, because in the prior question, the Pharisees tried to intimidate him by their claim to social and religious position. They had the official credentials and Jesus did not. But he was unimpressed with them, and their egos were crushed. The Pharisees were the "men" who could not sway Jesus, and now their disciples try to pick up the pieces.

So a new strategy is adopted – the matter of taxes. The Pharisees hate paying them, the Herodians insist on their payment. They come at Jesus from two different angles.

On the one hand, if Jesus says yes – it is right to pay taxes to Caesar – the Pharisees can call him a traitor to the nation. Surely, in their view, the Messiah would be an immediate political figure, overthrowing Caesar, and would in no way pay taxes to the one he had come to overthrow. Baruch knows the hypocrisy in this, since his fellow Pharisees pay taxes to keep their positions. But too, at this point, it appears they are losing their grip on the pretension of sincerity, in their desperation to prove Jesus not to be the Messiah. But specially too, they want to accuse Jesus of idolatry.

The denarius coin has a portrait of Tiberius Caesar on it, and on the reverse side it reads in Latin: "Tiberius Caesar, son of the divine Augustus." It is a claim to deity by the son of a false deity, and as Baruch considers this fact, his minds races to the language Jesus uses of himself as both Son of Man and Son of God. Baruch is still pondering what this means, but he also sees that

Jesus, in his identity, stands in stark opposition to the idolatry and politics of Caesar. *Is Jesus now about to make his political move and lay claim to David's throne?*

The Pharisees rationalize that the handling of this coin is the pollution of idolatry, and surely no Messiah would handle it. They think that if Jesus says yes to the payment of taxes, they can then accuse him of regarding Caesar as a god, accuse him of idolatry and discredit him in front of the people.

On the other hand, if Jesus says no to the payment of taxes to Caesar, the Herodians can accuse him of political insurrection and treason against Rome. They know that this possibility would then allow them to petition Herod to have Jesus crucified.

These co-belligerents had Jesus trapped, regardless of what he said, so they think. Baruch reads their pensive faces, as both parties await an answer, to find out which one of them would deliver the victorious blow.

At this point, Baruch notes how Jesus changes the tempo of the contest. He sees the eyes of Jesus look penetratingly, one at a time, and in larger sweep, into the eyes of Pharisaical disciples and the Herodians. He is in control as usual. This time, he also interweaves a statement and rhetorical question that judge the matter up front: "You hypocrites, why are you trying to trap me?" Jesus knows his enemies are growing in desperation, but more so, their hardened hearts are only growing harder.

Their hypocrisy is evident to all present. After all, they have already admitted it to his face – the Pharisees refusing one moment to admit the truth, and having their disciples flatter him as a truth teller the next. The Herodians are known thus far to have been working behind the scenes, awaiting their moment to pounce.

Jesus does not initiate these words of judgment. He gives them only in response to blatant hypocrisy, while at the same time still treating his enemies with respect, giving them opportunity once again to measure up to the truth. He gives them an open-ended hospitality to their questions, however motivated.

With his words exposing their entrapping intent, Jesus now appeals to a definition of terms: "Show me the coin used for paying the tax." Show the evidence in question so it can be mutually examined.

They bring him a denarius, and Jesus asks a question of obvious certainty to all involved: "Whose portrait this? And whose inscription?" This is also a question of authority. It is Caesar's portrait and his inscription, indicating ownership of the currency as head of the state that backs it up. As the Pharisaical disciples and Herodians give answer, they are morally trapped into owning the answer. Once again thought Baruch, *Jesus has done it!* With eyes wide open, Jesus walks into another trap, gives open-ended freedom and respect to his plotting adversaries to engage in honest rabbinic debate, and they only succeed at falling into their own trap. *When will they learn?*

"Then give Caesar what is Caesar's, and give God what is God's."

They stand there dumbfounded and amazed, astonished and silent, jaws open and nothing to say. Again, silenced.

Baruch ponders it more deeply yet. Whereas the disciples of the Pharisees and the Herodians conspire to trap Jesus in their idolatry of religious and political power, Jesus specifically calls them to consider the image of God.

The moment Jesus says "portrait" and "inscription," Baruch, and all his fellow Jews, immediately think of the opening pages of Genesis where man and woman are created in the "image" and "likeness" of God. He muses to himself: *We are God's portrait.* This language is driving far deeper than mere politics, and thus, it more powerfully challenges the idolatry of Roman political power. *Where is Jesus aiming?*

Baruch also considers the language of the Ten Commandments in the Law of Moses, where the making of idols is proscribed, in the face of all the pagan nations that make idols of animals and objects and persons in service to demonically driven political tyrannies.

These proxy Pharisees, students having already memorized the entire Tanakh, immediately know what Jesus is saying. And along with the Herodians, they know he is challenging their actual idolatry of the temple and political power. As Baruch heard Jesus say years earlier to the Pharisees in the grainfields, "I tell you that one greater than the temple is here." There are so many intersecting and swirling and integral ideas coming from the mouth of Jesus. Baruch continues to be compellingly drawn to this man, he is further amazed, and yet there are so many other questions to ask and consider.

In view of all he is learning in watching Jesus, Baruch paraphrases in his own mind what Jesus has just said to the disciples of the Pharisees: *If Caesar is so foolish to call himself a god and circulate a coin that says so, then give him back his portrait and folly. There is no fear in touching a coin of idolatry, since idols are nothing. Let's see what comes of his claim when he stands before the true God on the Judgment Day. If Ba'al is god, let him contend for himself. If Caesar is a god, let him contend for himself. In the meantime, it is no loss for a true worshiper of God to pay taxes. But most importantly, give God back his portrait – which is not your money inscribed with the name of a pretender, but your souls, which are made in God's image and are his true possession.*

This is a paraphrase of inescapably political language – the image bearers of God are given stewardship to rule the creation from the beginning, to set up and govern the family and social order. Rome stands against this authority, and here Jesus challenges it head on. Jesus has come to set up true rule in the face of false rule.

In view of the Herodians, Baruch paraphrases in his mind the sum of what Jesus has just said to them: *God is not interested in your money and politics, and the attendant idolatry. He does not want Caesar's image, or that of anyone or anything else. He wants you, the image-bearers of God; he wants your heart, soul, mind and strength. Nothing less.*

Jesus says yes to the payment of taxes, but too, the Pharisaical disciples fail to make him an idolater, and the Herodians fail to find him guilty of plotting treason. Their souls are ablaze with agendas foiled, hypocrisies exposed, wisdom spoken they cannot, will not grasp, and a sinking feeling that somehow Jesus has successfully undercut all their claims to authority. He has undercut the pretense of both temple and state, and Herod and Caesar are also being challenged by words and character that are above reproach.

Baruch understands something of it, but far less that what he knows is there. The enemies of Jesus stand there, mouths shut and agitating gestures decoupled, amazed. So they walk away through the crowds. Jesus begins again to teach the people.

Baruch wonders: *What comes next?* He listens to Jesus teach.

Chapter Seven

Theological Nitpicking

Baruch then takes time to wander through the crowd, pick up the chatter, and get some lunch, but always keeps an eye on Jesus. He has been present at five points of conflict between Jesus and his enemies – three years earlier in the Galilean grainfields and in the synagogue, two days prior when Jesus entered the city and was challenged concerning the language of the Son of David, one day prior on the matter of the authority of Jesus, and now on the question of paying taxes.

Then Baruch cannot miss the obvious – now making their way around the crowds toward Jesus is a procession of leaders from the Sadducee party. They come in a conspicuous display of their wealth, their culture and their privileged place on the Sanhedrin, their postures erect and their gaze above the din of humanity against which they fear to rub.

Baruch quickly moves to get within earshot of what he expected will be a dynamic interaction with Jesus.

"That same day the Sadducees, who say there is no resurrection, came to him with a question. 'Teacher,' they said, 'Moses told us that if a man dies without having children, his brother must marry the widow and have children for him. Now there were seven brothers among us. The first one married and died, and since he had no children, he left his wife to his brother. The same thing happened to the second and third brother, right on down to the seventh. Finally, the woman died. Now then, at the resurrection, whose wife will she be of the seven, since all of them were married to her?'

"Jesus replied, 'You are in error because you do not know the Scriptures or the power of God. At the resurrection people will neither marry nor be given in marriage; they will be like the angels in heaven. But about the resurrection of the dead – have you not read what God said to you, "I am the God of Abraham, the God of Isaac, and the God of Jacob"? He is not the God of the dead but of the living.' "

"When the crowds heard this, they were astonished at his teaching."

Baruch is delighted to watch this interchange. He knows the territory well, and has to admit to himself how happy he is to see Jesus put the Sadducees in their place.

The Sadducees do not really accept the whole Tanakh as the fully trustworthy Scriptures. When they hear the words, "It is written," just like Jesus has already used, they always have a little scoff in their souls. They are unlike the Pharisees, who at least have to stop and be momentarily accountable to what is written in the Law, the Prophets and the Writings.

The Sadducees place themselves above that recognition, denying the possibility of the resurrection and the existence of angels. They know this puts them at odds with the account of the tree of life in the Garden of Eden, and at odds with the relentless testimony of the Tanakh to the presence and ministry of angels in service to the Messianic line.

Their interest is not like that of the Pharisees, who are offended when Jesus does miracles on the Sabbath, and thus get into a tussle over the question of divine intervention along with that of Sabbath rules. The Sadducees keep far from the subject of such divine action, and keep safe within the confines of the intellectual issues they like to address. They are safe by using other points of reference.

As the Pharisees and Herodians have already been silenced by Jesus, the Sadducees see their opportunity with their theological agenda in the forefront. They figure if they can silence Jesus, they will be at the top of the heap in terms of theology, in contrast to the Pharisees; and they will separate themselves from those among their fellow Sadducees who are politically motivated Herodians.

The Sadducees seek to assert superiority in handling the Scriptures, and Baruch witnesses their nitpicking concerns. They bring up a question dealing with levirate marriage in the Law of Moses.

"If brothers are living together and one of them dies without a son, his widow must not marry outside the family. Her husband's brother shall take

45

her and marry her and fulfill the duty of a brother-in-law to her. The first son she bears shall carry on the name of the dead brother so that his name will not be blotted out from Israel."

Levirate marriage is part of a larger definition of the "kinsmen-redeemer" law. It envisions an unmarried man living in the same household with his brother and wife (as opposed to already having his own household as a married man), on land they both inherited from their father.

The Law of Moses holds in high regard the name and inheritance of all the Israelites, where the land would stay in each family line throughout the generations. This way there can be no centralization of top-down political power gained by amassing land. This is why the year of Jubilee was instituted, intended so that all land would be returned to its family lineage at least every 50 years. Beginning with Joshua, the political authority was found in judges, men, and along with Deborah in her time, who presided over a locally based and decentralized definition of power, and finally with Samuel, the last judge, who grieved when Israel clamored for a king like the pagan nations. Saul, as such a king, then presided over a top-down enslaving government.

Thus, as Baruch is well schooled in such a Hebrew community ethic, he knows a childless widow could keep the land in the name of her late husband by the graciousness of her brother-in-law. She has already left her father and mother and their land, joining her husband's inheritance. The first son would take on her first husband's name and inheritance in legal terms, with the second son receiving the birthright of her second husband, and biological father of both. Social cohesion, prosperity and individual identity were well balanced.

And the brother-in-law is normally glad to do so. He loses nothing, for he still rears his first biological son, and he gains the continuity of his late brother's name, indeed of their mutual family name tracing back to their own father.

In the book of Genesis, the story is told of Onan refusing to honor his late brother Er in levirate marriage to Tamar, and is judged accordingly. In the book of Ruth, when Ruth the Moabitess returns to Israel, recently widowed and with her already widowed mother-in-law Naomi, it is this same kinsman-redeemer law that leads to her marriage to Boaz. She thus becomes the great-grandmother of David, and hence a foremother to the Son of David.

As Baruch's mind rolls through this background knowledge in a moment, as the Sadducees bring their question up, he again realizes that percolating just below the surface of the debate is the question of the Son of David. Explicit and dangerous political language. Not that the Sadducees here, or the religious elitists before them have intended to do so. Rather, it is unavoidable when the biblical texts are considered. And remarkably, Jesus is in such control of the language of the debate, that even his enemies, in pursuing secondary questions to the matter of the Son of David, cannot escape making at least implicit reference to it.

The Sadducees know all this background material, they know Jesus knows it, and they draw on a rich tradition as they refer to the kinsman-redeemer law.

But too, the people see that this is a strained attempt, making an example of seven men in a row dying and leaving the same woman childless, in order to question the resurrection. This example is a reference to the book of Tobit, regarded by the Pharisees and the rest of the Jewish nation as apocryphal. It held no historical validity or scriptural authority. The Sadducees are thus speaking about, on the one hand, what Moses has taught, then on the other, going to a source outside the Tanakh in order to demean Moses, and hence, demean Jesus in his affirmation of Moses. They are grasping at a nitpicking concern not germane to either the question of the resurrection or the book of Tobit itself.

In the story, a woman named Sarah was "given in marriage to seven husbands, and before each marriage could be regularly consummated they had all been killed by the wicked demon Asmodaeus."

In his answer, Jesus is blunt – the Sadducees know neither the Scriptures, nor the power of God.

So Jesus speaks to them in terms they can understand. In referring to the God of Abraham, Isaac and Jacob, he says that these words of God are addressed to them as their descendants.

Baruch's head is again spinning, for many other sub-textual theological strains are revealing themselves.

Prior to the Babylonian exile, the Judahites and Israelites called God by his Hebrew name, Yahweh. In the Law of Moses, there is great emphasis on the name of Yahweh, and as distinguished from all the names of pagan deities.

But following the exile, and across the intervening centuries, the pronunciation of Yahweh's name was replaced by the word *adonai*, meaning "Lord." Whenever a Jew saw Yahweh in the text of the Tanakh, he would automatically pronounce Adonai instead. Among his colleagues, Baruch had participated in many debates as to why this was so. The lead argument was that Yahweh's name was too holy to be pronounced.

But how could this be the case? Baruch would always ask himself. If this were the case, why did it not say so in the Tanakh? His fellow Jews know that the change in speaking his name happened after the exile, and that the name of Yahweh was spoken before that. So Baruch thought: *When we say, "It is written," why do we not pronounce what is written?* Baruch is in a small minority in this regard, the question always remained, but given the monolithic Jewish practice, and the charge of blasphemy that would come his way, Baruch pronounced Adonai in public.

Thus, Baruch is immediately attuned to the language at play. Jesus uses the present tense "I am the God" which is the same language that Yahweh uses in his appearance to Moses in the burning bush, when he declares his name to be the I AM, to be Yahweh. When Jesus earlier quoted Isaiah and Jeremiah in stating, "My house," the underlying authority of Jesus, as the Son of God, as Immanuel ("God with us"), language also used in Isaiah, stood out. *Who is this Jesus claiming to be?*

The Sadducees want, so they think, the I AM of God – Yahweh Elohim who is the divine Eternal Presence. As Jesus gives them his presence, subtly tied it into the presence of the living God, and follows through with the simple conclusion that God is the God not of the dead but of the living, the whole power of the I AM hits them with full force at a level deeper than the intellect. Baruch does not fully grasp all this, but he senses it deeply, knowing all the pieces of the puzzle, but not yet knowing how to assemble it fully in his mind.

The Sadducees are speechless. If Yahweh is the present tense God of Abraham, Isaac and Jacob – the very forefathers to whom they claim allegiance – and if he is also speaking to them in the presence of Jesus, then the Sadducees cannot object to the resurrection without saying that God is a god of the dead, and/or that they themselves are dead people.

Again it happens! Baruch witnesses another trap laid for Jesus, only to become a trap for those who laid it.

Jesus is saying that God is the God of Abraham, Isaac and Jacob – present tense – because they are alive in God's presence awaiting the final resurrection of all the saints. Jesus again shows his dexterity in handling the Tanakh, and the proud Sadducees know they cannot dispute his knowledge.

The crowds are astonished, the Sadducees are silenced. Baruch stands there, himself with nothing to say, but his momentary loss of words is in delight, not anger and fear.

Chapter Eight

Theological Grandstanding

Baruch now finds himself stepping up to the moment.

He is standing near some of his Pharisaical colleagues, and they are talking about how they have a narrow opportunity to reassert themselves over the humiliated Sadducees.

They call Baruch over. His mind is already reeling from his constant trek across the pages of the Tanakh, in considering exactly who the Messiah is, and whether or to what extent Jesus measures up. He is persuaded in all he had seen so far, but still thinking.

So now he wonders: *What is their agenda, and how might it involve me?* They know the tension they have with Baruch, as Baruch has watched but not participated in their groupthink. But too, they still respect him as an expert in the law, and have run out of options themselves. They see how the dreaded question of the Son of David seems repeatedly to surface, and they need somehow to stay clear of it.

So they ask him, "Perhaps you can ask Jesus a question, as an expert in the law, one that somehow gets to the core, so that we can see if he really is the Messiah." Baruch knows they are being disingenuous. Namely, they are plotting that maybe this honest Pharisee, with an honest question, could somehow trip Jesus up. This is their momentary desperate hope. And if perchance it succeeds, not only can they prevail over the Sadducees and Herodians, but possibly draw Baruch into their orb as well.

Baruch is no fool, and he sees a possible trap for himself. Yet, he is emboldened in seeing Jesus reverse every trap that has been laid for him. And in Jesus, he has yet to find any fault, only great wisdom reflecting a grasp of the Tanakh he sees in no man.

He agrees, and he knows the exact question to ask that always separate the true from the false. His lifetime of training prepares him for this very moment, and if his grasp of the Tanakh is honest and truly expert, is about to find out.

Here are the parallel biblical texts of this moment:

———————

"Hearing that Jesus had silenced the Sadducees, the Pharisees got together. One of them, an expert in the law, tested him with this question: 'Teacher, which is the greatest commandment in the Law?' "

"One of the teachers of the law came and heard them debating. Noticing that Jesus had given them a good answer, he asked him, 'Of all the commandments, which is the most important?' "

———————

"Jesus replied: ' "Love the Lord your God with all your heart and with all your soul and with all your mind." This is the first and greatest commandment. And the second is like it: "Love your neighbor as yourself." All the Law and the Prophets hang on these two commandments.' "

" 'The most important one,' answered Jesus, 'is this: "Hear, O Israel, the Lord our God, the Lord is one. Love the Lord your God with all your heart and with all your soul and with all your mind and with all your strength." The second is this: "Love your neighbor as yourself." There is no commandment greater than these.'

" 'Well said, teacher,' the man replied. 'You are right in saying that God is one and there is no other but him. To love him with all your heart, with all your understanding and with all your strength, and to love your neighbor as yourself is more important than all burnt offerings and sacrifices.'

"When Jesus saw that he had answered wisely, he said to him, 'You are not far from the kingdom of God.' And from then on no one dared ask him any more questions."

———————

"While the Pharisees were gathered together, Jesus asked them, 'What do you think about the Christ? Whose son is he?'

" 'The son of David,' they replied.

"He said to them, 'How is it then that David, speaking by the Spirit, calls him "Lord"? For he says,

" ' "The Lord said to my Lord:
'Sit at my right hand
until I put your enemies
under your feet." ' "

"If then David calls him 'Lord,' how can he be his son?" No one could say a word in reply, and from that day on no one dared to ask him any more questions."

"The large crowd listened to him with delight."

Baruch, our plausible character, the honest Pharisee and expert in the law, the one who notices "that Jesus had given ... a good answer," not only to the Sadducees, but to everyone else, steps up to the plate and directly engages Jesus.

He has opportunity, with all his prior experiences in watching Jesus in mind, to ask the most important question of all, one of theological integrity and interpretive power for the whole Tanakh, for thus grasping who the Messiah really was.

But his fellow Pharisees internalize the question as a matter of theological grandstanding, somehow hoping that whereas Jesus has successfully wrestled out of smaller questions, he will now trip over the greatest one. They also internalize the expectation that the answer Jesus gives, by definition, is far removed from the specific Messianic question of the Son of David.

Baruch answers Jesus, now as his teacher, his rabbi, agreeing with Jesus on the identification of the most important command of all, to love God with our whole beings, and to love our neighbors as ourselves. Baruch adds that such love "is more important than all burnt offerings and sacrifices."

With these words Jesus is delighted. He knows Baruch has learned that to which the Pharisees in the grainfields were impervious. He knows that Baruch is an honest Pharisee, a man who loves mercy. "You are not far from the kingdom of God."

This is not what Baruch expected, and yet, it cannot be otherwise. What now must he do to make up the remaining distance to the kingdom of God?

His fellow Pharisees stand there, nothing more to say, and Baruch stands next to them, wondering what will happen next.

Chapter Nine

Back to Square One

So Jesus stands there (in humble confidence), the Pharisees stand there (in exposed hypocrisy, silenced), the large crowds stand there (in eager anticipation of what will happen next), and Baruch stands there (likewise in eager anticipation).

Jesus has given his enemies the freedom to test him at every level, and he knows that they know, as the crowds know, as Baruch knows, that they are at the dead end of their intellectual, moral and spiritual ability to invent new arguments.

Baruch notes the symmetry of the week. Jesus allows his enemies to take the issue away from its true focus, from the primary question to secondary ones, and now that their agenda is exhausted, Jesus is in undisputed control of the conversation, returning to the primary question.

There is no disputing the authority of Jesus in overturning the tables of the money changers and benches of those selling doves, and in the healing the blind and lame. The real question goes back to the objections of the chief priests and the teachers of the law against the crowds and children calling Jesus the "Son of David," the Messiah, the Christ. They have tried to have him silence this proclamation. So Jesus challenges their right to silence the children's Messianic praises of him, and he engages them in a contest of silencings, rooted in the quote from the eighth psalm.

Thus, Jesus returns to square one, and since the religious elitists object to him being called the Son of David, he asks the positive question about their views of the coming Christ – whose son was he? They know the answer, and Jesus knows they do.

Baruch reads the deeper fury in their souls. They give the answer of the Son of David, but hated doing so. Jesus' mastery of control continues. He appeals with an authority which his enemies cannot disagree – he cites the Holy Spirit speaks through David from the book of psalms.

The Pharisees give the right answer, and Jesus agrees with them. But then he follows with the final exposing question, more fully expressed in Baruch's mind as he fleshes out the theology: *How can David, speaking by the Spirit, call the Messiah his Lord if he is also his son? Can the same Messiah be both the Father of David and Son of David at the same time?*

Jesus chooses the beginning of a text where Yahweh is speaking to the Messiah, a point not in dispute with the Pharisees. As Yahweh continues to speak to the Messiah in the subsequent verses, he says that he will place the enemies of the Messiah under the Messiah's feet.

Baruch notes that this is the first time Jesus actually mentions the word "enemy" in the face of his enemies, using the quote of a Messianic prophecy to do so. Jesus now makes explicit the words from the eighth psalm they first quoted in their minds two days earlier – when they had finished a sentence of the psalm Jesus had deliberately left incomplete – "because of your enemies, to silence the foe and the avenger."

Baruch sees further depth here too. In this final referenced psalm of David, the Hebrew text says "Yahweh said to my Lord." Jesus is giving reference to God the Father speaking to Jesus as the Son of God, as the Lord of David, which strongly hints at Jesus' claim as the Messiah to be Immanuel, God with us in the flesh. Jesus asks his enemies how the Messiah can be both the Father of David and Son of David at the same time. Namely, the God whose strength is greater than the universe is the same God whose strength is manifest in the Son of David who uses the strength of childlikeness in the face of human pretense.

And with the quote of this psalm, it is obvious to Baruch and the crowds that Jesus is declaring publicly that he has won the debate. His enemies are self-silenced – they are now under his feet.

In their debate that week, the chiefs priests sought to insinuate that Jesus is no greater than the pagan deity Ba'al. Jesus here again refutes this idea. The Messiah is both Lord of David and his Son at the same time. How could this be? Yet this is what the Scripture says. No one has an answer. Baruch thinks his mind cannot spin anymore, but here it goes again. He knows he has much more study to do, that his expertise in the law is quite modest in reality. *What is next?*

Chapter Ten

Judgment and the Authority to Die

He does not have to wait long. Baruch notices that the crowds have grown in size. The chief priests, the Pharisees, their disciples, the elders of the people, the Herodians and the Sadducees are also there. They have all been jostling with each other in competition to silence Jesus, but as well, they have all been hoping dearly that at least someone would put this rabble rousing itinerant wannabe rabbi and wannabe Messiah in his place. Now they can only stand and listen, hoping perhaps, somehow, that Jesus might trip himself up.

"Then Jesus said to the crowds and to his disciples: 'The teachers of the law and the Pharisees sit in Moses' seat. So you must obey them and do everything they tell you. But do not do what they do, for they do not practice what they preach. They tie up heavy loads and put them on men's shoulders, but they themselves are not willing to lift a finger to move them.' "

Baruch has seen Jesus show his enemies incredible honor, and he sees how he first practices what he preaches. Jesus wishes for the elites to be true elites, instead of joining with the Romans to tyrannize the all in service to their own top-down control. And yet here, where Jesus can easily claim political authority as the Son of David, he has yet to do so. Instead of calling for revolt against hypocrisy, he calls the people to honor something higher, while at the same time now beginning to aggressively cut down his enemies in the spiritual and moral realms.

" 'Everything they do is done for men to see: They make their phylacteries wide and the tassels on their garments long; they love the place of honor at banquets and the most important seats in the synagogues; they love to be greeted in the marketplaces and to have men call them "Rabbi." ' "

" 'But you are not to be called "Rabbi," for you have only one Master and are all brothers. And do not call anyone on earth "father," for you have one Father, and he is in heaven. Nor are you to be called "teacher," for you have one Teacher, the Christ. The greatest among you will be your servant. For whoever exalts himself will be humbled, and whoever humbles himself will be exalted.' "

Baruch himself is a member of the elite, but he has distanced himself from the elitists, and has been told by Jesus that he is not far from the kingdom of God. He considers: *What does it mean to be a true elite, one who sits in the seat of Moses to govern the Jewish people, one who is worthy of the honor of such a role, one who enters the kingdom of God?*

He sees the contrast that Jesus defines, and eschews in his soul all the trappings of power into which his fellow Pharisees embrace. But he is also a rabbi, a father and a teacher, so what is the nature of Jesus forbidding the further use of this language? It is language rooted in the Tanakh. Perhaps the key is in understanding the contrast between honorable and humble function, and the idolatrous attachments to which many of his colleagues cling.

Jesus now turns to a wholesale rebuke of the Pharisees and teachers of the law:

– Woe to you hypocrites who shut the kingdom of heaven in men's faces – you yourselves will not enter it! Woe to you hypocrites who labor to win a convert, only to make him twice as much a son of hell as you are! Woe to you blind guides who make foolish oaths and an idol out of the temple! Woe to you hypocrites who tithe but neglect justice, mercy and faithfulness – who strain at a gnat and swallow a camel! Woe to you hypocrites who cleanse the outside of the cup and dish, but inwardly are full of greed and self-indulgence! Woe to you hypocrites who look outwardly beautiful like a whitewashed tomb, but inside are full of dead men's bones and all uncleanness! Woe to you hypocrites who build tombs to honor slain prophets, whom you yourselves would have also slain! –

" 'You snakes! You brood of vipers! How will you escape being condemned to hell? Therefore I am sending you prophets and wise men and teachers. Some of them you will kill and crucify; others you will flog in your synagogues and pursue from town to town. And so upon you will come all the righteous blood that has been shed on earth, from the blood of righteous Abel to the blood of Zechariah son of Berekiah, whom you murdered between the temple and the altar. I tell you the truth, all this will come upon this generation.'

" 'O Jerusalem, Jerusalem, you who kill the prophets and stone those sent to you, how often I have longed to gather your children together, as a hen gathers her chicks under her wings, but you were not willing. Look, your house is left to you desolate. For I tell you, you will not see me again until you say, 'Blessed is he who comes in the name of the Lord.' "

With the debate over, Baruch watches Jesus pass judgment. He has always held back from this, but now the time has come. *Has the time also arrived to take political authority?*

So much more to consider.

As Jesus uses the language of hell, it directly refers to the Valley of Ben Hinnom. This valley, outside Jerusalem, is where the trash dump continually burns, and where leading up to the Babylonian destruction of the city, the Jews had descended into the practice of child sacrifice some 600 years earlier.

Thus, this is a major metaphor that defines what hell means for the Jews, and more powerfully yet for the Pharisees and teachers of the law who despise mercy and the praise of the children. Jesus calls his self-silenced enemies "sons of hell," the most damning of language.

Then here, at the end of this delivered judgment, Jesus quotes a messianic psalm, "Blessed is he who comes in the name of the Lord." Baruch again notes the symmetry of these several days. Jesus has come full circle from when the people shouted it when he first entered the city.

These words are powerfully central to the Hebrew people and Messianic expectations. They are also said at Passover, and here Jesus is giving his last words to his enemies before leaving the temple. He is saying, at least in part, that they will not see him again until they cite these very words at Passover. Jesus is in control of his schedule, and here, it seems, in Baruch's mind, that much more is to unfold before he can grasp the question of politics in the face of the Roman Empire.

Namely, he has heard about how Jesus has taught often about his suffering, death, resurrection and a second coming. Baruch does not fully understand it, and he sees in Jesus all the power and authority necessary to drive out the Romans and set up the kingdom of God, now, in Jerusalem. Yet too, he considers language from the suffering servant sections in the prophet Isaiah. From the first servant song, he recites to himself:

Here is my servant, whom I uphold,
  my chosen one in whom I delight;
I will put my Spirit on him
  and he will bring justice to the nations.
He will not shout or cry out,
  or raise his voice in the streets.
A bruised reed he will not break,
  and a smoldering wick he will not snuff out;
he will not falter or be discouraged
  till he establishes justice on earth.
In his law the islands will put their hope.

He sees in Jesus a man who brings justice first to the needy and dispossessed people on-on-one, being very gentle and innocent with those seeking mercy. And too, he sees in Jesus a man who has shrewdly dealt with his plotting enemies, and in the end, following their chosen silence and hatred of mercy for the needy, he judges them without mercy.

Is it really possible that this man does not intend to take political authority now, and that somehow the elitists will succeed in petitioning Rome to crucify him as an insurrectionist? That he will rise from the dead, just as he did for Lazarus, and then come again to set up his rule?

In thinking about these details, and the nature of death on a Roman cross, Baruch now recites to himself the fourth servant song from Isaiah:

See, my servant will act wisely;
*   he will be raised and lifted up and highly exalted.*
Just as there were many who were appalled at him –
*   his appearance was so disfigured beyond that of any man*
*   and his form marred beyond human likeness--*
so will he sprinkle many nations,
*   and kings will shut their mouths because of him.*
For what they were not told, they will see,
*   and what they have not heard, they will understand.*
Who has believed our message
*   and to whom has the arm of the LORD been revealed?*
He grew up before him like a tender shoot,
*   and like a root out of dry ground.*
He had no beauty or majesty to attract us to him,
*   nothing in his appearance that we should desire him.*
He was despised and rejected by men,
*   a man of sorrows, and familiar with suffering.*
Like one from whom men hide their faces
*   he was despised, and we esteemed him not.*
Surely he took up our infirmities and carried our sorrows,
yet we considered him stricken by God,
*   smitten by him, and afflicted.*
But he was pierced for our transgressions,
*   he was crushed for our iniquities;*
the punishment that brought us peace was upon him,
*   and by his wounds we are healed.*
We all, like sheep, have gone astray,
*   each of us has turned to his own way;*
and the LORD has laid on him
*   the iniquity of us all.*
He was oppressed and afflicted,
*   yet he did not open his mouth;*
he was led like a lamb to the slaughter,
*   and as a sheep before her shearers is silent,*
so he did not open his mouth.
By oppression and judgment he was taken away.
*   And who can speak of his descendants?*

For he was cut off from the land of the living;
  for the transgression of my people he was stricken.
He was assigned a grave with the wicked,
  and with the rich in his death,
though he had done no violence,
  nor was any deceit in his mouth.
Yet it was the LORD's will to crush him and cause him to suffer,
  and though the LORD makes his life a guilt offering,
he will see his offspring and prolong his days,
  and the will of the LORD will prosper in his hand.
After the suffering of his soul,
  he will see the light of life and be satisfied;
by his knowledge my righteous servant will justify many,
  and he will bear their iniquities.
Therefore I will give him a portion among the great,
  and he will divide the spoils with the strong,
because he poured out his life unto death,
  and was numbered with the transgressors.
For he bore the sin of many,
  and made intercession for the transgressors.

Baruch has the whole Tanakh memorized, and it is easy to recite portions on a moment's notice when some even modest cross-reference triggers a connection, whether alone or with his colleagues. And here it is triggered. And a thousand new questions flood his soul. *What now is in front of me? Where now does Jesus go? What are the authorities plotting?*

And yet, here is Jesus, at the end of his words, publicly lamenting for Jerusalem and those who have decided to kill him. Jesus, in the face of his plotting enemies, still loves them.

Baruch is still in his tense but respectful relations with his fellow Pharisees. He posed exactly the type of question they hoped he would at the end of the debate, but it did not accomplish their purposes. Thus, Baruch has access, but not completely, to what the enemies of Jesus are up to.

He learns of a meeting planned.

"Then the chief priests and the elders of the people assembled in the palace of the high priest, whose name was Caiaphas, and they plotted to arrest Jesus in some sly way and kill him. 'But not during the Feast,' they said, 'or there may be a riot among the people. ' "

Baruch knows Caiaphas, and the machinations of his father-in-law Annas, behind the scenes, where both essentially share the power of the office of high priest. The word reaches Baruch that the prior week Caiaphas spoke at a meeting of the Sanhedrin, saying that Jesus should die at the hands of the Romans, so that the whole Jewish nation would be spared. Namely, a scapegoat.

Baruch is restless for the next day, as more rumors swirl. Late that evening he hears of Jesus being arrested in Gethsemane, and guessing what is afoot, he rushes to the house of Caiaphas, and in non-descriptive clothing. As he does so, he notices some members of the Sanhedrin arriving ahead of him, and in the darkness of the hour, Baruch decides not to make himself known. He keeps in the shadows outside the courtyard. He finds a position where he can see into a corner of the room where Jesus is surrounded by his accusers.

The chief priests are bringing various witnesses to accuse Jesus, but they prove unsatisfactory. Finally two men accuse Jesus of planning to destroy the rebuild the temple in a matter of three days. Baruch has heard this before in the chatter, but too, he knows that Jesus may have been talking about the temple of his own body, at least as one friend had reported it to him.

"Then the high priest stood up and said to Jesus, 'Are you not going to answer? What is this testimony that these men are brining against you?' But Jesus remained silent.

"The high priest said to him, 'I charge you under oath by the living God: Tell me if you are the Christ, the Son of God.'

" 'Yes, it is as you say ... But I say to all of you: In the future you will see the Son of Man sitting at the right hand of the Mighty One and coming in the clouds of heaven.'

"Then the high priest tore his clothes and said, "He has spoken blasphemy! Why do we need to hear any more witnesses? Look, now you have heard his blasphemy. What do you think?'

" 'He is worthy of death,' they answered.

"Then they spit in his face and struck him with their fists. Others slapped him and said, 'Prophesy to us, Christ. Who hit you?' "

Baruch sees so much coming together. It is almost surreal, and the darkness of the night is more than just physical – an encroachment seeking to get inside the fibers of the soul. The chief priests on the day of Yom Kippur, in the autumn, are to select the most spotless one-year old male lamb from the herds of Judah, to be the annual atonement sacrifice for the sins of the whole nation. The chief priests are to examine the lamb in the presence of the people, examining every inch of the lamb's body for even the slightest defect.

Yes, Baruch has heard about John the Baptist calling Jesus the "Lamb of God, who takes away the sin of the world!" But so much he has not understood until now. But especially, he considers Jesus. He was examined by the chief priests and all his enemies in public, and found blameless. Baruch also thought of the fourth servant song in Isaiah that speaks of the Messiah who "was led like a lamb to the slaughter, and as sheep before her shearers is silent, so he did not open his mouth." Jesus has already answered the chief priests in public, so now he chooses to be silent in the face of their newest cooked up accusation. He only answers when Caiaphas requires of him an oath. Jesus is in control, even in the face of what now seems to be unavoidable death. *So much yet to understand.*

The morning dawn now begins to suggest itself over the eastern sky. After sunrise, Baruch sees Jesus being led out, bound, with the chief priests and some elders of the people, along with some soldiers, leading the way. They take him to the palace of Pilate, the Roman governor. Baruch keeps his distance, preferring anonymity in this dangerous and unpredictable hour.

Pilate holds a trial of sorts, and then suddenly Jesus is rushed out to another location. Baruch follows at a distance, and it leads to a meeting with King Herod, who happens to be in town. Baruch does not get close enough to hear the trial, but it ends quickly and Jesus is led back to Pilate's palace.

A mob is growing outside the palace, and Baruch notes the chief priests and elders rounding it up from among the city's most lawless people.

"Now it was the governor's custom at the Feast to release a prisoner chosen by the crowd. At that time they had a notorious prisoner, called Barabbas. So when the crowd had gathered, Pilate asked them, 'Which one do you want me to release to you: Barabbas, or Jesus who is called Christ?' For he knew it was out of envy that they had handed Jesus over to him.

"While Pilate was sitting on the judge's seat, his wife sent him this message: 'Don't have anything to do with that innocent man, for I have suffered a great deal today in a dream because of him.'

"But the chief priests and the elders persuaded the crowd to ask for Barabbas and to have Jesus executed.

" 'Which of the two do you want me to release to you?' asked the governor. 'Barabbas,' they answered.

" 'What shall I do, then, with Jesus who is called Christ?' Pilate asked.

"They all answered, 'Crucify him!'

" 'Why? What crime has he committed?' asked Pilate.

"But they shouted all the louder, 'Crucify him!'

"When Pilate saw that he was getting nowhere, but that instead an uproar was starting, he took water and washed his hands in front of the crowd. 'I am innocent of this man's blood,' he said. 'It is your responsibility!'

"All the people answered, 'Let his blood be on us and on our children!'

65

"Then he released Barabbas to them. But he had Jesus flogged, and handed him over to be crucified."

Baruch sees Jesus as he is led back into the governor's palace, and as he comes out with a twisted circle of thorns pounded into his skull, with blood streaked across his face. Baruch follows the gathering crowd as Jesus is led forth by the soldiers, under the heavy weight of the cross bar.

Baruch knows that the Messiah will reclaim rightful political authority for the nation. But too, he now reflects on some words his colleagues reported to him, when they were debating Jesus earlier: "The reason my Father loves me is that I lay down my life – only to take it up again. No one takes it from me, but I lay it down of my own accord. I have authority to lay it down and authority to take it up again. This command I received from my Father."

Jesus is in control, he has judged his enemies, and now he is exercising his authority to die for the nation.

Chapter Eleven

Reflections

Baruch thinks through all he has seen as he follows the crowd through the city and outside its walls. He reflects on Jesus in his mind:

- *Jesus loves mercy, and opposes the hypocrites who hate mercy.*

- *Jesus accepts the mantle of the Son of David, the Messiah, as especially given him by the children.*

- *Jesus nonetheless does not take political power.*

- *Jesus opposes the idolatry of the temple, and the state, among the religious and political leaders.*

- *Jesus both quotes and fulfills many Messianic prophecies.*

- *Jesus uses rabbinic skill, with moral innocence and shrewdness, to avoid all the traps set for him by his enemies, to turns them back on his accusers.*

- *Jesus is fully hospitable to the toughest questions of his enemies.*

- *Jesus cannot be trapped on questions of the Sabbath, his authority, paying taxes to Caesar, the question of the resurrection, and he answered my question concerning the greatest commandment.*

- *Jesus thus gets his enemies to silence themselves in public debate.*

- *Jesus controls the whole debate, and brings it back to his agenda – who is the Son of David?*

- *Jesus then judges his enemies publicly and they have no answer.*

- *Jesus is proven blameless in the sight of his enemies as he now heads to certain death on a Roman cross, and that blamelessness has been purchased by giving hospitality to the toughest questions of his self-pronounced enemies.*

- *Thus, Jesus has taken authority to die as the Lamb of God!*

Baruch also sees all the elements of the fourth servant song Jesus has fulfilled. *How will the pending ones still come to pass?*

As he follows the rolling mayhem outside the city, he still wonders how this pending death will translate into the coming of the kingdom of God. Jesus did say, he has learned, that a central element of prayer is to say: "Your kingdom come, your will be done, on earth as in heaven." *Now as well as then?*

How will the death of Jesus lead to genuine political justice and mercy for all the nations? *This is the promise of the Messiah, is it not? Jesus, in the face of his enemies – does this spell a prelude to something dynamic in grappling with these questions? The resurrection? Another coming?*

Jesus told Baruch him that he is not far from the kingdom of God. He has to find out the answers to so many questions …

Content of Book Two: The Text

Introduction

A Dangerous Book

This modest book is dangerous, and the challenge is to honestly profile a difficult balance. Namely, Jesus gives comfort to the needy, while being shrewd with self-aggrandizing elitists.

This book is also written for serious readers able to carve out some time for undivided attention, for readers who can thus pay attention to human nature in the midst of hope and conflict.

And as serious readers grasp the difficult balance, a prelude to a godly political reformation will be seen.

Elitists are found across human history and civilizations. "Elite" is a good word that refers to taking special skills and using them to bless others. "Elitists" are those who pollute such skills in a selfish capacity; they are a very small number of people whose identity is to rule over others, and to cling to that power no matter what.

Jesus is a danger to elitists in his very nature, while also weeping over their folly. He will not put up with their wickedness. Rather, his purpose is to embrace, lift up and save all who suffer under their false power – under the false power of the ancient serpent always lurking in the background. And yet, his invitation to all elitists, to choose life, is never off the table so long as they have the breath of life.

In Book One, my purpose was to invite us inside the most crucial storyline ever; and here in Book Two, we take a step back to look at the biblical text in more detail.

Can we imagine ourselves in Jerusalem the week leading to the crucifixion of Jesus? Can we imagine looking into his eyes, as he looks into the eyes of his friends and enemies alike, and grasp his very person? Do we know Jesus, and not merely know about him? If so, then perhaps the balance of his comfort and shrewdness can be understood.

The Power of Psalm 8

As I write about elsewhere, I grew up in an agnostic Unitarian context, was always drawn to the beauty of the universe and the wonder of life, and ran into the supernatural presence of God as a 14-year old in 1967. Such wonder is beautifully portrayed in Psalm 8, and I have always loved it.

In 1984, as a married man with a growing family working my way through Gordon-Conwell Theological Seminary, I arrived at my last course in the M.Div. program – exegesis in the Hebrew poets with Dr. Doug Stuart, chairman of the Old Testament department.

"Exegesis" is a term that refers to digging into the sources to discover what is there. And to do exegesis in Hebrew poetry required all the academic skills we had thus far learned. We were limited to 10 verses of text to translate and exegete, and I readily chose Psalm 8. Here is the text, in the New International Version (NIV):

O LORD, our Lord,
    how majestic is your name in all the earth!

You have set your glory above the heavens.
From the lips of children and infants you have ordained praise
    because of your enemies, to silence the foe and the avenger.

When I consider your heavens, the works of your fingers,
    the moon and the stars, which you have set in place,
what is man that you are mindful of him, the son of man that
    you care for him?

You have made him a little lower than the heavenly beings
    and crowned him with glory and honor.

You have made him ruler over the works of your hands;
    you have put everything under his feet:
all flocks and herds, and the beasts of the field,

the birds of the air, and the fish of the sea, all that swim the
paths of the sea.

O LORD, our Lord,
how majestic is your name in all the earth!

There are some translation issues here for the academic reader. But let me just note two that affect my conversion, and how crucial Psalm 8 will prove to this book.

I always translate "LORD" from the original Hebrew, *Yahweh*. Indeed, the Hebrew for the Lord God, *Yahweh Elohim*, refers to he who in his essence is greater than space, time and number – the only written concept in human history that contemplates and defines such a reality: "I AM WHO I AM." Jesus took this name to himself (I AM) thirty-one times in the Gospel of John. Thus, from my very starting point of faith, I was contemplating the essence of Yahweh Elohim, of Jesus as Yahweh in the flesh, before I knew him.

As well, the word translated "praise" is actually "strength" in the Hebrew, and this balance will prove to be the most crucial hinge point that shows the balance of who Jesus is in the face of his friends and enemies.

But I did not know these elements when I chose to exegete the psalm in 1984. What I knew was the beauty of gazing into the night sky and seeing God's handiwork. It contemplates the awe of our existence in the face of a beautiful nighttime vista of the heavens, and considers who we are in God's sight. This proves to be the essence of childlike faith.

And too, there is that one confrontational clause, indicating that the praise of the children will silence those who prove to be the enemies of the Gospel. Conflict in the midst of beauty – why?

Chapter One

Why Did Jesus Have Enemies?

Who is Jesus?

Character is revealed in the face of conflict, and the gospels reveal Jesus most clearly in the face of his enemies.

How is it that a man who heals the sick and raises the dead would have enemies to begin with? Why would these religious and political enemies track his every move once he announces himself? Why would he be a threat to the status quo? What is the nature of his threat?

Once on the Sabbath, Jesus and his disciples are in the grainfields, picking some heads of grain for their meal. They are taking advantage of the Law of Moses that provides for the edges of the fields not to be harvested, allowing the poor access to food. Jesus and his disciples have no regular income, and are provided for at other times by some wealthy women disciples, or here, by going into the grainfields. They are the poor.

The Sabbath is the day of rest, given to all people since creation. But the religious legalists in the days of Jesus twist its purpose. Instead of a day of rest for body and spirit, they seek to impose a set of unbreakable rules on the whole Jewish population, giving them a straightjacket instead.

So as the disciples are picking some heads of grain to eat, all of a sudden some Pharisees "saw this" and criticize them for breaking the Sabbath.

Now, how does this scene unfold?

The Bible is an exquisite set of short stories within the grand historical narrative, beautifully constructed and written for people who know enough to imagine themselves inside a given storyline. All the stories of the Bible are uniquely true, and the truth is dynamically grasped as the readers see how the stories represent reality. This is the case, not only in terms of factual elements, but also at the deeper level, namely, the portrayal of human nature.

Hence, "Jesus, in the face of his enemies," is not only the telling of factual history, but especially, it is a study in human nature as Jesus interacts with men and women with their varieties of agendas, hopes and fears.

Can we imagine ourselves as onlookers as this scene unfolds?

Does a group of the Pharisees merely happen to pass by and see Jesus and his disciples from a distance?

Or are they part a posse that follows Jesus around – trying to keep inconspicuous – but while watching his every move? Then suddenly they see the violation of their Sabbath rules. They run across the field and come up to him, catching their breaths in order to catch the "lawbreakers."

Or are they closer at hand the whole time? Here, Jesus might instruct his disciples to pay them no heed, as they say no in their spirits to the intimidating shadow stalkers, knowing that conflict will soon follow.

Or, perhaps we can imagine the well dressed Pharisees, suddenly popping up from their hidden positions behind some stalks of grain, with fingers wagging, "Gotcha!"

Regardless, they are tracking his every move, and Jesus answers them. He tells them how David once entered the house of God, with his companions, and ate some consecrated bread – an "unlawful" act. But they were hungry and on a mission approved by God. Something deeper is at play.

Jesus continues, "Or haven't you read in the Law that on the Sabbath the priests in the temple desecrate the day and yet are innocent? I tell you that one greater than the temple is here. If you had known what these words mean, 'I desire mercy, not sacrifice,' you would not have condemned the innocent. For the Son of Man is Lord of the Sabbath" (Matthew 12:5-8).

In other words, Jesus is using some precise sarcasm in saying that the priests desecrate the Sabbath in fulfilling their prescribed duties according to the Law of Moses. The Pharisees are thus hypocritical in order to maintain their position that it is unlawful to pick heads of grain on the Sabbath. Their laws about the Sabbath reflect a legalistic view of sacrifice and religion, and an attempt to control the lives of others. These are elitists who are happy to condemn the innocent in order to maintain their social positions. Their "proper" ritual sacrifices trump mercy. It is a mercy to which Jesus is inviting them, even as he boldly responds to their initiative of confrontation.

As well, Jesus makes an understated Messianic claim that "someone" greater than the temple is present, and a third person reference to the Son of Man as Lord of the Sabbath. He is speaking this to Jewish elitists who should have readily understood who he was.

Jesus does not have enemies because he chooses to live the life of the poor and glean for a meal. Jesus has enemies because he has the "audacity" to demonstrate the authority to "speak truth to power."

Immediately after this conflict in the grainfields, Jesus goes into a synagogue and meets a man with a shriveled hand. The Pharisees "were looking for a reason to accuse Jesus, so they watched him closely to see if he would heal him on the Sabbath" (Mark 3:2).

In other words, the enemies of Jesus are on the prowl to find excuse to accuse him, and this prowl is profiled relentlessly across the four gospels. They are even willing to condemn a crippled man in the process.

So Jesus addresses this conflict head on, and calls the man to stand up in front of the whole assembly. Jesus is face to face with his enemies, as his eyes meet their eyes, the eyes of the crippled man and the eyes of all the onlookers. In this pregnant moment, for perhaps a few seconds, Jesus looks intently, assesses the situation and the human souls being laid bare.

Can we imagine ourselves in this assembly? What would have been our response?

Jesus then says to his self-chosen enemies, the "experts" in the law: "Which is lawful on the Sabbath: to do good or to do evil, to save life or to kill?" (v. 4).

They have already criticized Jesus on what is lawful in the grainfields, and now they stand there to accuse him of violating the Sabbath if he does the "work" of healing on that day. They are willing to crush the innocent and hungry in the name of the "law," to forbid healing in the name of the "law," and to maintain the proper legal "sacrifice" of worship on the Sabbath. But all the while they despise acts of mercy, all the while in order to hold onto their self-aggrandizing power.

This is why Jesus has enemies – the One who has come to set things straight. This is why Jesus has enemies – they were those who held elitist power and mouthed the care for the poor and sick, but always acted in self-interest.

Jesus now ups the ante – he frames it as a matter of good versus evil, the saving of life versus murder. Surely the religious elitists would choose the good and life. "But they remained silent."

"He looked around at them in anger and, deeply distressed at their stubborn hearts, said to the man, 'Stretch out your hand.' He stretched it out, and his hand was completely restored. Then the Pharisees went out and began to plot with the Herodians how they might kill Jesus" (vv. 5-6).

Can we imagine the intensity, the heat of Jesus' angry eyes?

Jesus undercuts his enemies at the level of the human conscience. In his presence, their souls are publicly unmasked, not only for hypocrisy in matters of the law, but to show that the Law of Moses is only a pretext for them. They do not care for the poor and sick, as does the Law of Moses, they do not choose the good and life for others, as the Law of Moses calls them to do. Instead, they trample whomever to get whatever they want, and here plot to kill Jesus for his interference in their wickedness.

In one more of many instances, a crucial conflict emerges in Matthew 19:1-9. The Pharisees seek to twist the Torah to justify divorce "for any and every reason." Jesus thus challenges them, "Haven you read?" Namely, they are the educated religious leaders, and Jesus holds them to account. He then appeals to the biblical order of creation where the marriage of man and woman is ordained, and never to be broken.

The Pharisees come back seeking shiftily to say Moses "commanded" divorce, and Jesus answers I saying that Moses only "permitted" in the case of "marital unfaithfulness." Not "for any and every reason" as it were.

Why did Jesus have enemies? The answer is plain to see for those who want to see it.

Chapter Two

The Power of the Level Playing Field

The Love of Hard Questions

As we seek to grasp the storyline text of Jesus in the face of his enemies, we will do so principally in the Gospel of Matthew, written for a Jewish audience with a generous amount of Messianic quotes from the Hebrew Bible. And we will do so with a focus on Passover week just prior to the crucifixion.

The most important debate in human history occurs during this week. Jesus is confronted by his sworn enemies, and in response, he provides them a level playing field to rake him over the coals with their toughest questions. When all was said and done, his enemies choose to silence themselves in his presence, to the delight of thousands of common people who observe great spontaneous theater.

Here we witness a radical theological idea – the power of a level playing field, where informed choice and the love of hard questions can flourish. It has deep roots back to the Garden of Eden, where Yahweh Elohim places good and evil, life and death, freedom and slavery, side-by-side for man and woman to choose between.

The Son of David

The Gospel of Matthew focuses on two crucial themes – the Son of David and the strength of childlikeness. This balance is crucial for us to understand who Jesus really is.

The first theme begins in the first verse of Matthew: "A record of the genealogy of Jesus Christ the son of David, the son of Abraham ..."

"The Son of David" is a Messianic title. The term "Messiah" comes from the Hebrew *mesheach* and means the "anointed one," the one who is anointed to be king. The Greek term for Messiah is *christos*, from which we derive the

"Christ." It occurs 25 times across the Bible, ten of which are strategically found in Matthew's gospel.

Thus, as we consider the Christ as the Son of David – we see the radically political nature of such a title. Matthew starts his gospel by declaring Jesus to be the Son of the founding King of Jerusalem, David, tracing back 1,000 years. Jesus is the anointed heir. This proclamation is made directly in the face of the rulers of Jewish Palestine under Caesar – whether Herod the Great at the time of Jesus' birth, known as "king of the Jews" (gained through marriage and treachery), or one of his sons, Herod Antipas, tetrarch at the time of Jesus' crucifixion.

The Herods are fearful because the Son of David is coming to reclaim a stolen kingship. Herod the Great seeks to kill Jesus as an infant, and Herod Antipas succeeds several decades later, by proxy, if but for a short weekend.

Yet the Jewish political zealots do not find in Jesus what they are hoping for. They yearn for a political messiah who would immediately overthrow Rome – but Jesus' agenda is far larger, and accomplished in two comings, not one. Namely, in his first coming, Jesus comes as the Suffering Servant. He gives of himself completely so that all humanity may receive the invitation to become citizens in the kingdom of God.

Then, once that invitation becomes truly universal, Jesus returns a second time as the conquering King – human kingdoms come to an end, and the eternal kingdom of God arrives where "There will be no more death or mourning or crying or pain, for the old order of things has passed away" (Revelation 21:4). The Prince of Peace reigns.

The Strength of Childlikeness

The second crucial theme in Matthew's gospel is the strength of childlikeness. This theme percolates from Matthew 1:18 at the birth of Jesus, until Passover week.

In Matthew 18-20, just prior to Jesus entering Jerusalem, this theme is prominent. Jesus teaches his disciples that the nature of the kingdom of heaven is for people to "change and become like little children." He gives positive definition to childlikeness: "Therefore, whoever humbles himself like this child is the greatest in the kingdom of heaven." He also gives warning to those who would injure the faith of a child, and rebukes the disciples for their instincts to prohibit the little children from coming to him.

Greatness is found in humility, and strength is found in the childlikeness of awe, wonder, innocence and trust. Little children, beginning in the womb, intrinsically know how to trust the good until they suffer violation as they grow up in a broken world.

Shrewd Yet Innocent

Once, Jesus teaches his disciples how to behave in the face of the enemies of the Gospel: "I am sending you out like sheep among wolves. Therefore be as shrewd as snakes and as innocent as doves" (Matthew 10:16).

As we see Jesus, the Son of David, employing the strength of childlikeness, we note this balance between shrewdness and innocence. In Psalm 18:25-26, we read: "To the faithful you show yourself faithful, to the blameless you show yourself blameless, to the pure you show yourself pure, but to the crooked you show yourself shrewd." Jesus proves to be both innocent and shrewd, both friend and foe – depending on how he is regarded.

The prologue to John's gospel states: "the light shines in the darkness, but the darkness has not understood it" (1:5). The Greek term for "understood" is *katalambano*, which literally means "to reach up, grab hold, seize power, dethrone, cast down and trample," or most simply, "to overcome."

By definition in physics, ethics and spiritual domains, darkness flees the light. That which is both shrewd and innocent cannot be understood by the darkness, and thus cannot be overcome, for it cannot overcome what it does not understand. Jesus is the Light of the world, and Satan, as the prince of darkness, cannot understand the combination of shrewdness and innocence.

Biblically, there is the power to live in the light and the power of the level playing field, both of which are shrewd yet innocent.

Chapter Three

Setting the Stage for the Necessary Contest

Entry into Jerusalem

With an understanding of the Son of David and the strength of childlikeness, we are able to see how these issues dominate the debate Jesus has with his enemies during Passover Week.

On the first day of the week (Palm Sunday), several hundred thousand Jewish pilgrims, along with many God-fearing Gentiles, begin to stream into the city that normally has some 80,000 residents. Jesus has just raised Lazarus from the dead, the word has gone out, and the crowds that are following Jesus continue to grow. They accompany him as he approaches Jerusalem from his years in the countryside.

Thus, we read in Matthew's gospel:

> As they approached Jerusalem and came to Bethphage on the Mount of Olives, Jesus sent two disciples, saying to them, "Go to the village ahead of you, and at once you will find a donkey tied there, with her colt by her. Untie them and bring them to me. If anyone says anything to you, tell him that the Lord needs them, and he will send them right away."

> This took place to fulfill what was spoken through the prophet:

> "Say to the Daughter of Zion,
>   'See, your king comes to you,
> gentle and riding on a donkey,
>   on a colt, the foal of a donkey.' "

> The disciples went and did as Jesus had instructed them. They brought the donkey and the colt, placed their cloaks on them, and Jesus sat on them. A very large crowd spread their cloaks on the road, while others cut branches from the trees and spread them on

81

the road. The crowds that went ahead of him and those that followed shouted,

"Hosanna to the Son of David!"

"Blessed is he who comes in the name of the Lord!"

"Hosanna in the highest!"

When Jesus entered Jerusalem, the whole city was stirred and asked, "Who is this?"

The crowds answered, "This is Jesus, the prophet from Nazareth in Galilee" (21:1-11).

This first portion of the Passover week storyline shows a people who understand the language of the Son of David. The reputation of Jesus is reaching its apex as he times the moment of his entry into Jerusalem, Messianic fervor is high, and many people think the Messiah will immediately overturn Roman political power. But Jesus has no intent to take human political power. He is the kingly contrast to Herod, but his purposes are far deeper.

The Start of the Messianic Prophecies

If we were watching Herod Antipas enter Jerusalem in 30 A.D., we would see him mounted on a prize war stallion, prancing in pride, or perhaps on a chariot, wearing his royal garments of one sort or another, with trumpets and a unit of soldiers that would shove people out of his way as they lay down a royal carpet, as they announce the "greatness" of the coming "king" (though technically a tetrarch, a lower status), and as the people are required to give deference and praise.

In contrast, as Jesus approaches Jerusalem, we witness him riding a young donkey led by its mother, symbolic of a king who is among the people as a citizen, and not over them as a military conqueror. Matthew here quotes from Zechariah 9:9, the first of nine Messianic prophecies fulfilled as Jesus enters the city and debates his enemies. Messianic prophecies date back to the Garden of Eden, where the promised Messiah is to come through a chosen lineage.

This contrast is unmistakable in the minds of the people – those who suffer under Rome's yoke, who have endured many "triumphal" military entrances of Herod and others into the city. Jesus chooses to ride on the humble cloaks of his disciples, and the cloaks are also the carpet of the common people along with the cut palm branches, thrown down in spontaneity. His humility is the opposite of Herod or Caesar's pretense, and the result is the freely chosen praises of the people, young and old.

We have already noted the long running conflict between Jesus and his enemies. As well, there is a conflict with Herod, but at a different, less direct level. First, Jesus' cousin, John the Baptist, challenges Herod concerning incest – as Herod had forcibly taken his brother's wife for his own. This gets John thrown into prison and eventually beheaded.

Second, several days before Passover week, some Pharisees come to Jesus and try to scare him away from coming to Jerusalem, warning that Herod wants to kill him. Here, Jesus makes his most explicit statement concerning temporal politics – "Go tell that fox, 'I will drive out demons and heal people today and tomorrow, and on the third day I will reach my goal.' In any case, I must keep going today and tomorrow and the next day – for surely no prophet can die outside Jerusalem!" (Luke 13:32-33).

A fox is one who steals and kills the baby chicks for a meal. Jesus then gives a cry, "O Jerusalem, Jerusalem, you who kill the prophets and stone those sent to you, how often I have longed to gather your children together, as a hen gathers her chicks under her wings, but you were not willing! Look, your house is left to you desolate. I tell you, you will not see me again until you say, 'Blessed is he who comes in the name of the Lord' " (13:34-35).

Jesus set himself up as the defender against the intruding predator, as a hen protecting her chicks, Jesus against Herod, humility against pretense – while still lamenting for his enemies as he is also aiming well past Herod in his purposes.

This brief vignette from Luke's Gospel helps to set up what we see in the text of Matthew's storyline – namely, fulfilled Messianic prophecies. When the people shout their praises, they call out "Hosanna to the Son of David!" "Hosanna" is a term of praise that means "Save!" This is a clear reference to Psalm 118:25; and the Book of Psalms is Israel's hymnbook. This is the second Messianic prophecy Matthew cites, followed by a third Messianic prophecy in the next verse in Psalm 118, which Luke quotes Jesus himself saying several days earlier: "Blessed is he who comes in the name of the Lord."

Thus, the whole city is stirred, while multiple tens of thousands of pilgrims are streaming into it. The reputation of Jesus for his ministry in the countryside in the preceding years is well known. Now, with Lazarus having been raised from the dead, and Jesus entering the city en route to the temple, the Messianic fervor is exploding.

Imagine the intensity of feelings at this moment. Over seven centuries earlier (721 B.C.) most of the nation of Israel was carried away into Assyrian captivity, having forsaken the Law of Moses. These Israelites were assimilated into the pagan nations in the subsequent years, including the Samaritans in the days of Jesus. The only portion of ancient Israel remaining after the Assyrian conquest was Judah (the Jews) and some others who assimilated into Judah.

Then the Jews lost the city of Jerusalem and the temple 135 years later (586 B.C.) when Yahweh Elohim allowed their sins to be judged by the Babylonian conquest, destruction and exile. They had forsaken the true worship of Yahweh, with its mercy and justice for all people equally, and in its place worshiped idols alongside Yahweh, descending into the practices of sorcery, sacred prostitution and child sacrifice. The attempt to worship both pagan idols and Yahweh was a "mixing of opposites" – the classic definition of "syncretism."

The temple has been rebuilt in modesty since, at Yahweh's directive. But apart from a period of independence, the Jews are otherwise occupied by various foreign powers that do not regard Yahweh as the true God.

They yearn for freedom from the boot of Roman oppression, and here is Jesus – with authority, miracles and words of comfort. He comes into the city as the Son of David, fulfilling well-known Messianic prophecies. The zealots in their midst expect a political victory then and there. But Jesus has deeper priorities.

Chapter Four

Contest Engaged

False Separation Between Church and State

In Jerusalem at the time of Jesus, there was a false separation between religion and politics ("temple and state" or "church and state" as it were).

The majority of the Jewish religious leaders had compromised with the Roman authorities in this matter. Rome was adroit in its treatment of its conquered people. It did not seek to wipe out their leadership per se. Rather it sought to bring them into the Roman political order, and give them the temple as a vested interest, a bribe, not to rebel against Rome if external or internal threats ever arose. This strategy was central to Rome's long-term political success as an empire, one that was reaching its height at the time of Jesus.

The Jewish people were also a great thorn in Rome's side, not sharing the pagan assumptions of polytheistic Rome, as did other subjects. And they more passionately resisted (sometimes in bloody clashes) the imperial cult of Caesar, and likewise gained exemption from military conscription – the only people conquered by Rome able to do so.

So Rome went out of its way to cultivate within the Jewish religious elite a political alliance. Herod the Great had Edomite lineage (tracing back to Israel's brother, Esau), and he ruled Jerusalem and Judea from 37 B.C. to about the time of the birth of Jesus. His wickedness was well known in palace intrigues and ruthlessness with his enemies.

Idolatry of the Temple

Herod loved architectural magnificence, and in 20 B.C. he initiated the rebuilding of the Jewish temple originally built by Solomon over 900 years earlier. He did so according to its original grandeur, and as a means to seduce the Jewish religious elite to support, or at least not revolt against his political tyranny.

Solomon's temple was destroyed in 586 B.C. because the Jews had made an idol out of it; namely, they ultimately worshiped the temple instead of Yahweh for whom the temple had been originally built. This idolatry of the temple surfaces again and again as Jesus challenges his enemies, and is powerfully in play when Jesus says to the Pharisees in the grainfields that "one greater than the temple is here," namely, him.

In 20 B.C., the religious elite were seduced by idolatry once again, the promise of a restored temple, if they would but forfeit the Law of Moses in one crucial arena – political authority beyond the temple walls. They were allowed to have their religion, but only if confined. They were allowed to have the Law of Moses, so long as it was not fully the Law of Moses.

On these terms, they were allowed to have the temple, and all the income it produced for them. If they violated these boundaries, Rome would crush the nation, city and temple. This was the fear of the elitists, for in Jesus claiming to be the true king, the Son of David, he is a great threat to their economics.

The Jewish elitists were also allowed to have their sacrifices and other rituals serve as outward symbols. This too Jesus threatened, for they had hollowed out the purposes of the original sacrificial system, even as the common people yearned for its original substance. Jesus is coming to make the true sacrifice. Their annual sacrifice of a lamb for the sins of the nation (Yom Kippur – the Day of Atonement) is going to be once and for all fulfilled in himself as the Lamb of God.

This is why most of the Jewish religious elite are the principal enemies of Jesus, more deeply than Herod. As blood is thicker than water, their religion holds a far deeper allegiance than that of temporal politics.

Judgment Begins With the Household of God

When Jesus comes into Jerusalem on Sunday of Passover week to the Messianic shouts, he is allowing the people to proclaim him Lord over both temple and state. The true Messiah is a threat to the false separation between temple and state, not because he is coming to change the temporal political order per se. Rather, he is coming first to change the hearts of the people and the nature of the covenant (believing) community, out of which flows the larger social transformation, ultimately aiming at the eternal kingdom of God. It is the Pharisees, Sadducees, teachers of the law, elders, priests and scribes who thus become the first line of battle against the Messiah. This is a multi-layered Jewish leadership, often at cross-purposes with itself, but overwhelmingly against Jesus as a threat to their established status quo.

The text continues in Matthew 21:12-13:

> Jesus entered the temple area and drove out all who were buying and selling there. He overturned the tables of the money changers and the benches of those selling doves. "It is written," he said to them, "My house will be called a house of prayer,' but you are making it a 'den of robbers.' "

When Jesus enters the city, he goes straight to the temple area, which is known as the "Court of the Gentiles." This is the place where pagan people are welcome to come and seek the God of Israel, without first having to undergo circumcision and other requirements to become Jewish. It is an area roughly equal in total space to seventeen football fields (26.2 acres) during Solomon's days, but is now far larger and still in the process of being enlarged. Though Herod's temple was built in 20-19 B.C., the much larger temple courts he envisioned are not completed until 63 A.D., just before Emperor Titus burned it all to the ground in 70 A.D.

The Gentiles do not have to be "ritually clean" when they come into the outer court, as is required for Jews in the inner courts. In the outer courts there are Jews making money at usurious rates from the purses of fellow Jews. During the annual Passover week, Jews from the whole nation and the Diaspora (those dispersed among pagan nations) come to Jerusalem 1) to pay the annual temple tax; 2) to offer personal sacrifices according to the Law of Moses for their own sins; and 3) to celebrate the Passover meal, which includes the ritual slaughter and eating of the paschal lamb, commemorating the Israelite deliverance from Egypt under Moses.

Those who have traveled a long distance, and specially those among them who are poor, cannot bring their sacrifices with them. Thus, Jewish entrepreneurs set up animal pens, and cages with doves, or pigeons, to sell to the travelers. The doves are the least expensive and usually serve as the offering of the poor. The sellers charge far more than is normally the case, taking advantage of the moment. The temple tax has to be paid in the local Tyrian currency.

Thus, travelers are especially vulnerable, and the money changers charge unjustly high rates. The complaint of Jesus is not against the honest business of selling animals for sacrifice, or even the practice of local currency requirements that need money changers. His judgment is against those who take advantage of others with unfair business practices. As well, they should do their business, in honest terms, outside the temple walls. Inside the temple walls there is far greater, even religious, pressure for the people not to complain about the prices.

While this activity was going on, Jesus enters the city to the Messianic shouts and praises, and "the whole city was stirred." The common people yearn to see him, to hear him, to be healed, to see the enemies of Israel vanquished and the kingdom restored. But the ripple effect of his entry also notifies all the elitists, from the Pharisees who had warned him, to Herod, to all between including the military leaders. Everybody is talking about the rabbi from the countryside, his reputation, and wondering what will happen next. The common people know the elitists hate Jesus and will try to kill him. The elitists fear the common people. So everywhere in the city and its environs, the chatter is whispered in corners of fear or wonder, and jubilantly expressed in places of hope.

Imagine the money changers and those selling the sacrificial animals. They are terrified about what might happen to their business. If Jesus gets the Roman authorities angry enough, Herod will send in soldiers and shut down Passover week (he commands five cohorts, about 5,000 troops). The Jewish businessmen will suffer much financial loss, perhaps their largest portion of income for the year. But too, they are Jews, and they know they are ripping off fellow Jews in the name of religion, and their consciences are rattled with an impending if undefined judgment coming their way.

This "gentle king" Jesus is coming, with thousands following him, straight to their place of business. The noise grows as a wave of humanity approaches behind this man. There are already thousands of people in the Court, including those lined up to pay their temple tax or purchase their doves or larger animals, and those performing their sacrifices across the courtyard at the times of evening and morning sacrifice. This "gentle king" is not so gentle with the "den of robbers."

We can readily imagine the benches of those selling doves, just inside each of the ten gates, several to one side; and to the other side, several tables of the money changers. In John's gospel, Jesus is also reported to have done this once before, near the beginning of his ministry (2:12-16). Here we also see the details of the cattle and sheep also being sold, likely in their stalls nearby, and of Jesus using a whip of cords made on the spot. He is furious at the sight of true Jewish faith being polluted by Jewish businessmen engaged in ripping off fellow Jews.

If Jesus again uses such a cord in the final conflict during Passover week, imagine the perspective of the merchants as he comes their way, snapping the whip and saying, "Get these out of here!" They have to make a quick and desperate calculation, for this is the worst of both possibilities.

First, they are being ordered to close down business as the Romans might do if they shut down Passover week altogether. But the Romans might also have allowed them to take their doves and animals with them, and gather their sacks of various coins before leaving. And second, they are being chastised with a Messianic prophecy by the Messiah, he is angry, their consciences are pricked, and they have no time to collect their possessions.

They are forced to flee, but no further away than they can manage, always looking back at what is happening to their possessions. If they are selling birds or livestock, they watch their benches being overturned one after the other, landing hard against the stone pavement. Their animals are thus agitated by the commotion, wings flapping and the grunting and kicking against their confines. On top of this, Jesus halts all related business in this de facto bazaar (see Mark 11:16).

90

And too, the money changers watch as Jesus approaches their forcibly abandoned tables. Behind them are many sacks of coins from various nations in the Diaspora from which so many Jews have traveled. They and their colleagues do business with many tens of thousands of households, changing the foreign coins into Tyrian coins at usurious rates. Their tables have neat piles of gold, silver, copper and other coins.

After a Jewish pilgrim has done business with them, he turns to go across the courtyard with his family, to the imposing temple (some fifteen stories high) to pay the annual tax. He has to negotiate his way among the people giving their evening or morning burnt offerings, with the smell of blood and smoke charging the atmosphere.

We can imagine Jesus as he extends his arms and hands from his robe, sweeping the piles of coins onto the uneven pavement, and they roll as far as the pavement allows. The common people see this money from where they stand at a distance, and they can imagine how one gold coin is worth half a year's wages. Then the money changers see Jesus grasp the rear corner and front leg of a table, still with some coins on it, to lift the back forward and as it thuds hard on the stone pavement.

Imagine too, these arms and hands of a carpenter grabbing the work of a carpenter, laying hold of the best quality tables as the money changers are wealthy. And Jesus, in his apprentice years, made the best of the best.

Imagine the perspective of Jesus in this action – not against any person, but against the ill-gotten gain of hypocrites who are serving to mock the name of the Lord in the presence of Gentiles – the very reason why the Jews lost the nation and temple in 586 B.C.

Jesus now has the complete attention of the thousands of people there, and declares, "It is written ..." With these opening words, the whole crowd quiets immediately, even the displaced merchants. The Jews know well the Hebrew Scriptures from childhood, and the Gentiles present are seekers of the God of Israel as the true God, and they are also oftentimes well versed in the Hebrew Bible. Too, they are looking for the Messiah, and have heard or are among those who had shouted Messianic prophecies moments earlier. They all know that when these words are stated, the written Word of God is about to be quoted.

"My house will be called ..." The people are poised for a Messianic prophecy to be fulfilled (the fourth in Matthew's text), and as soon as the first few quoted words are uttered, the majority of them know what words are to follow. They know exactly where in the scroll of Isaiah these words are to be found. And as well, Jesus melds them with words from Jeremiah 7:11 (the fifth Messianic prophecy here).

If Christians today, as well as others, were to hear two words spoken in public, "Our Father ... ", we would know what is to follow. In Jesus' day, as he utters these two words, "My house ..." (it is one word in the Hebrew and Aramaic), the people know what is to follow: "It is written," he said to them, " 'My house will be called a house of prayer,' but you are making it a 'den of robbers.' "

In Mark 11:17, Jesus quotes the full text from Isaiah along with Jeremiah 7:11: "Is it not written: 'My house will be called a house of prayer for all nations?' But you have made it 'a den of robbers.' "

In the earlier words recorded in John 2:16, Jesus stated the same judgment in his own words: "Get these out of here! How dare you turn my Father's house into a market!"

Also, in this singular moment, we can imagine the common people hearing Jesus' words as spoken by God incarnate – speaking Yahweh's very words, with the same authority that Isaiah recognized when Yahweh spoke them to him. "My house" is being spoken by its owner, present in the flesh.

For the common people, this is the Good News of the Savior. But for the religious elitists, this is blasphemy – or they have to rationalize it as such in order to resist obeying Jesus. The common people are overjoyed, but the elitists are infuriated. And all those within hearing range are listening closely as the following words come forth. The house of prayer for all the nations has been perverted into a "den of robbers," and the Messiah is come to pronounce judgment on this state of affairs.

In the Law of Moses, the Israelites are told clearly that they are the covenant community of Yahweh, and that their deliverance from slavery in Egypt is an act of Yahweh's grace. They are the remnant people through whom the Messiah is to come for the whole world. As such, the Israelites are held to a higher accountability than that of the surrounding pagan nations. The Israelites are to be an example to the pagan nations, and are given blessings if they obey Yahweh's goodness, but also warned of the curses that will land on them if they disobey and instead follow pagan ethics and customs – especially idolatry, sorcery, sacred prostitution and child sacrifice.

But Israel and Judah disobey repeatedly, ignoring the warnings of the prophets. This leads to the Assyrian and Babylonian exiles.

As Jesus comes to the rebuilt temple during Passover week, he comes in judgment. Judgment begins with the household or family of God (see 1 Peter 4:17). After this encounter, having given the Jewish elitists and their followers an opportunity to repent, he makes the judgment clear in Matthew 23:37-24:2:

> "O Jerusalem, Jerusalem, you who kill the prophets and stone
> those sent to you, how often I have longed to gather your children
> together, as a hen gathers her chicks under her wings, but you were not
> willing. Look, your house is left to you desolate. For I tell you, you
> will not see me again until you say, 'Blessed is he who comes in the
> name of the Lord.' "

> Jesus left the temple and was walking away when his disciples
> came to him to call his attention to its buildings. "Do you see all
> these things?" he asked. "I tell you the truth, not one stone here will be
> left on another; every one will be thrown down."

This jumps ahead of the text, but shows Jesus' trajectory. We have already seen how Jesus likewise lamented over Jerusalem in Luke 13:34-35 with these exact same words.

The money changers and those selling doves or livestock are guilty of the full weight of the sins of Israel and Judah up to this moment when Jesus clears them out of the temple area. Not only are they ripping off fellow Jews, but they are also doing so in the presence of Gentiles coming to the temple to seek the true God. In Matthew's gospel, the focus is on a Jewish readership; but in Mark's gospel where the focus is on a Gentile readership, he includes the full quote of Jesus regarding a house of prayer "for all nations," for all "peoples," for the "Gentiles." The Messiah is called to be "a light for the Gentiles" (Isaiah 42:6), and he comes first to the Jews to be the sacrificial paschal lamb of God, and then in the power of his death, resurrection and ascension, he gives his Spirit to empower his disciples to bring the Good News to all the world (see Acts 1:1-11).

This is why the gospels record no opposition to Jesus when he does this act. The money changers do not try to protest – they know they are guilty. The religious elitists do not protest – they know they are guilty at a deeper level, prostituting their teaching and leadership offices for their own power, in their twin idolatries of the temple and politics. But the common people love it. The One who has just been hailed as the coming Messiah is behaving like the Messiah – cleansing the house of God as his first act upon entering the city.

Contest engaged.

Chapter Five

Falling Into Their Own Trap

Judgment and Mercy

The text continues in Matthew 21:14-17:

> The blind and the lame came to him at the temple, and he healed them. But when the chief priests and the teachers of the law saw the wonderful things he did and the children shouting in the temple area, "Hosanna to the Son of David," they were indignant.
>
> "Do you hear what these children are saying?" they asked him.
>
> "Yes," replied Jesus, "have you never read,
>
> " 'From the lips of children and infants
>   you have ordained praise'?"
>
> And he left them and went out of the city to Bethany, where he spent the night.

Repeatedly in the Bible we see the themes of judgment and mercy side by side.

Here, as Jesus executes judgment on the usurious merchants and their supporting structures, mercy is what follows. When oppressors and hypocrites are judged, those who suffer under them rejoice, for in their sufferings or social dispossession, they know their sins and needs. So in this moment, the blind and the lame come to Jesus at the temple itself, recognizing his authority, and they are healed. But the chief priests and teachers of the law become indignant at the response of the children who begin to shout "Hosanna to the Son of David."

There are four factors that come together at this point.

First, Matthew cites the use of the Son of David as especially found on the lips of the dispossessed, the blind, mute, foreigners, demonized and now the little children.

Not only are the blind and lame healed – those who in prior times have not been welcomed into the temple area – but now they follow Jesus in. And it is too much for the elitists to see the sight of these little barefooted urchins, as it were, the children of the common people, calling for the stuff of political rebellion in naming the Son of David. The chief priests, et al., become indignant. These children have witnessed their parents calling Jesus the Son of David. Now that they witness the authority of Jesus in the face of hypocrisy, along with his power to heal the blind and the lame, they repeat with enthusiasm what their parents have taught them. He is behaving just like the Messiah is supposed to behave.

Second, the religious elitists fear that these children could spark a riot, and therefore the Romans would come and destroy the temple, even the nation. Just after Lazarus is raised from the dead, the religious elitists know they cannot deny such a miracle, and thus their last resort is to plot how to kill Jesus so as to avoid such Roman judgment (see John 11:45-57). The Pharisees and chief priests call a formal meeting of the Sanhedrin – the Jewish ruling council permitted by Rome to address internal matters – for this purpose.

The battle lines are drawn, his enemies define themselves, and Jesus shrewdly prepares for his entry into the city. The Sanhedrin wants to arrest him before he is able to publicly teach, preach and heal inside the city or in the temple area. The Pharisees have already tried to scare him away. They are all governed by the fear of losing the temple and city, and the privileged positions they hold due to this "separation of temple and state" arrangement.

Thus, Jesus strategically withdraws briefly, perhaps to the desert regions, and from there begins his walk into the city on Palm Sunday. As he starts out, it is not long before he is spotted, the word spreads like wildfire, people follow him and the numbers grow dramatically.

Third, the role of the chief priests is crucial, at the beginning of the debate, and after its conclusion. They represent a select few, who by the first century A.D. have the same rigorous training as all rabbis ("teachers of the law"). At age four, all Jewish boys are started in learning the Hebrew Bible (the "Tanakh," a Hebrew acronym for the Law, the Prophets and the Writings). From that point forward there is a winnowing process until adulthood (about age 13), when the best candidates are put on track to becoming rabbis, which takes until age 30. This is a culture where the average lifespan is maybe 40, but those wealthy enough (a small minority) to have clean water, good food and some competent attention by physicians, along with other basic amenities, live longer, often into their 60s or better.

The chief priests are usually men of at least 50 years, and have professionally reached the highest echelon of stature and power. Part of their duties involve the examination of the sacrificial lamb on the Day of Atonement (Yom Kippur, in the fall) in public for any defects. Passover is in the spring, the first of seven annual feasts in the Jewish calendar, and Yom Kippur is the sixth. Jesus is aiming to die on Passover, but also in fulfillment of the purposes of Yom Kippur.

Though the Sanhedrin is plotting to kill Jesus, they fail to prevent his public appearance. So they follow every move of Jesus once he enters the city, looking for their opportunity to arrest him out of sight of the people. The chief priests are leading the way, with a cadre of other teachers of the law in tow. But their elitist indignation gets the better of them, and they react to Jesus when he demonstrates his powerful balance of judgment and mercy. They do not like the "wonderful things he did," and when the children erupt in praise of the Son of David, they explode publicly and directly against Jesus.

And fourth, the chief priests and teachers of the law pride themselves in their knowledge of the Tanakh. If they are asleep, upside down like a bat in its cave, and are poked and asked to recite the Scriptures, they can do so at any point required, forward and backward, in Hebrew, Aramaic and Greek. They live and breathe the words of the Hebrew Bible, but here they refuse to honor the Word in the flesh (see John 1:1-14).

So their indignation flares into the open as the common people shout Messianic phrases, and as Jesus quotes Isaiah and Jeremiah in clearing the temple area. Jesus does so while consciously fulfilling these Messianic Scriptures, and the chief priests and teachers of the law have one motivation at this point – to disprove Jesus, to prove their self-assumed superiority in handling the Scriptures. Thus, they only need to trip Jesus up once, and then they can dismiss him theologically, dismiss him as a pretender and not the real Messiah, and focus on a pretense to have him arrested for a political crime. Some months earlier Jesus had rebuked a group of Pharisees while having dinner with them, and thus "the Pharisees and the teachers of the law began to oppose him fiercely and to besiege him with questions, waiting to catch him in something he might say" (Luke 11:53-54).

The religious elitists are thinking continually on how they can trip Jesus up in his words. Jesus willingly walks into this trap, but on his own terms of knowing the Messianic prophecies completely, whereas in their pretense, they are blind to the truth of the Tanakh they study so much.

Thus, to have the despised blind and lame people healed, and to have the despised little children start shouting "Hosanna to the Son of David," they see their whole house of cards is about to topple if the crowds were to call for Jesus as King over and against king Herod. They are scared as deeply as possible. They hate mercy, and resist judgment. The table is set for the true power contest.

The Strength of Childlikeness Employed by the Son of David

In their indignation, the chief priests and teachers of the law challenge Jesus with an edge of insult, asking him, "Do you hear what these children are saying?" Now, is it possible Jesus did not hear? No. So this is not their real question. As well, Jesus has just healed the blind and lame – in their presence. His power in miracles is not enough to bring them to repentance, for the will must be engaged, and they are unwilling. Jesus has also healed many deaf people in his ministry, and the religious elitists know this well.

The Bible is full of humor, but all humor is a creature of culture, and it is the art of surprise. As well, it works far better in conversation than in the written text, where eyeball-to-eyeball interaction is in place. This is why many jokes fail when translated, or when delivered in cross-cultural contexts.

Part of biblical humor, including its use of puns, is found in adversarial contexts such as Jesus is now facing, and becomes sarcasm, a truly difficult genre to use well. When Elijah confronts the false prophets of Ba'al years prior, we read the following:

> Then they called on the name of Baal from morning till noon, "O Baal, answer us!" they shouted. But there was no response; no one answered. And they danced around the altar they had made.

> At noon Elijah began to taunt them. "Shout louder!" he said. "Surely he is a god! Perhaps he is deep in thought, or busy, or traveling. Maybe he is sleeping and must be awakened." So they shouted louder and slashed themselves with swords and spears, as was their custom, until their blood flowed. Midday passed, and they continued their frantic prophesying until the time for the evening sacrifice. But there was no response, no one answered, no one paid attention (1 Kings 18:26-27).

One pun in use is the Hebrew word translated as "waver," earlier in v. 21, where Elijah asks the Israelites how long they will "waver" between Yahweh and Ba'al, as he calls on them to make a choice. When the prophets "danced" around their altar, calling on Ba'al to answer them, the same word is in place, which literally turns into a "limp" with all the bloodletting and sapping of strength that follows.

In our text here, we can see the nature of Elijah's taunts to elitists who had chosen to follow the witch Jezebel, rather than follow Yahweh who had delivered the Israelites from slavery in the Exodus.

Elijah is exposing the de facto non-existence of their god Ba'al. Thus Elijah, in this vein of serious humor, wonders if Ba'al does not answer because a) he is deep in ponderous thought, concentrating so hard that he cannot hear the pleas of his devotees; b) he is otherwise busy; c) he is traveling, i.e., too far away to hear the calls; or d) he is so deep in sleep that he cannot hear their desperate cries for help. Now the NIV and other translations are too modest, literally, when their translations say Ba'al might be "busy." In the Hebrew the word means literally "to relieve oneself," thus, Elijah is mocking a false god as one stuck in the outhouse, indisposed and unable to give answer until he finishes his "business."

Note how the bitter edge of the enemies of Jesus focuses on asking him if he "hears." Their sarcasm is dripping with hatred. No doubt part of the background of this question is the attempt on the part of these religious elitists to turn the tables on Jesus. They know Elijah's taunt, they are doing their best to disprove Jesus as the Messiah, and here they challenge him with a sub-textual innuendo, with a taunt that he is no better than the pagan god Ba'al – unable to hear. They are desperate, trying to insinuate, "You are no better than a pagan deity!" But this is a false use of the Scriptures, as the devil did in tempting Jesus in the wilderness, and they know it.

Also, and at a deeper level yet, they are not just asking a question, but making a demand: "Shut them up! Shut the children up because they could provoke a riot, and Rome will come and destroy our temple and nation." This is their real fear, as well as the loss of a large source of their income.

Jesus knows all this. So here the text shows how Jesus simply answers, "Yes." And as he does, we can readily imagine a smile in his facial expression. He loves his enemies and wants for them reconciliation with God, and he has the self-confidence to show some light-heartedness while being serious. He labors for this to the end of the age for all people, but at the same time he will not allow confirmed and stubborn enemies to hinder the proclamation of the Good News to the needy, or to other enemies who may repent and believe. The only people who can give a genuine smile (not a condescending smirk) in the face of conflict are those who are at peace with themselves, and confident in God's grace that what they are about is the pursuit of truth and mercy.

Jesus continues, and poses his question in response, "have you never read ...?" One reason it is easy to imagine the smile on Jesus' face is the opposite nature in his use of a return sarcasm. His enemies are sarcastic in an attempt to destroy him in their insecurities and fear. They mock his ability to hear, he who has healed the deaf. Jesus, loves them in the hope they will humble themselves, repent and join the kingdom of God, but nonetheless treats them as adults. They who have read and memorized the entire Tanakh better than the rest of Jewish society, are asked by Jesus not only if they have read, but how deeply, how well to they actually know what is in the text. Their purposes in precise sarcasm are of different purposes.

The chief priests and teachers of the law are now burning with anger, as Jesus honestly turns the tables on their dishonest attempts to turn the tables on his acts of mercy. They set a trap for him, the trap fails, and they are about to step into it themselves. They know he hears what the children are saying, and he knows they have read the Scriptures inside out better than virtually anyone else. We can imagine, that as they set the table, Jesus smiles easily, asks them a question, their pride is incited, and they are doubly motivated to prove him wrong. "Of course we have read the text! We know it better than anyone else. Who do you think we are? We are educated at the best rabbinic schools in Jerusalem, and you are but an uneducated rabble rouser from the northern countryside next to the Gentiles!" (Or to put it in modern American slang, "a hick from the sticks.") The pain of tragicomedy throughout.

Yet these words, as it were, whether outwardly expressed or inwardly fuming, ring hollow in their souls. They know they cannot contest the teachings of Jesus nor how the common people respect his true authority. As well, they certainly cannot challenge the reality, the facts, of his many miracles. But Jesus is probing deeper to see if they understand the text. He asks them if they have read a section from Psalm 8 (the sixth Messianic prophecy Matthew cites here): " 'From the lips of children and infants you have ordained praise ...' "

This is quoted from the Septuagint (LXX), which is the Greek translation of the Hebrew Bible between 284-246 B.C., by some seventy Jewish scholars, with excruciating faithfulness in how to render the text from Hebrew to Greek.

But especially, Jesus does something shrewd and powerful – he stops the quote in the middle of the original grammatical sentence, focusing on the positive elements of the children's praise in giving answer. The chief priests and teachers of the law know he stops the sentence mid-stream. Jesus leaves it to them to fill in the negative reality that is to follow – the reality that they are his self-chosen enemies.

So, returning to our earlier observations about the people's automatic response when Jesus says, "It is written ..." and "My house ...," where they know what is to follow, it is more so the case with the religious elitists here. They know the text by heart, and as Jesus stops in the middle of the sentence, what do they do? They automatically continue, in their minds, with the rest of that sentence of the Messianic prophecy, if not more. Jesus deliberately causes this to happen. The whole grammatical sentence reads: "From the lips of children and infants you have ordained praise because of your enemies, to silence the foe and the avenger."

Here we see who Jesus is in the face of his enemies.

This is the most powerful and defining moment in the conflict between Jesus and his enemies. Let's unpack the components.

First, the Hebrew word of Psalm 8:2, translated in the Septuagint translates as "praise" is *oz*, a simple word meaning "strength." Now why is this? Translation is an art and not a mathematical science. The purpose is not to make a wooden rendering of words as atomistic (stand-alone) units, but to show their part in the grammatical sequence. In Hebrew, context modifies the translation of a given word, so in Nehemiah 8:10, as the Jews were rebuilding their destroyed city walls in the face of relentless threats from their enemies, Governor Nehemiah says, "... the joy of the LORD is your strength."

Here, "strength" is not from the Hebrew word *oz*, but another word, meaning a place of safety against the enemies (which is the nature of the wall they are rebuilding). Context is key, and all these ideas converge – joy and safety, praise and strength. So in the Septuagint, the *oz* or strength of children is represented by praise (the children shouting, even singing, to Jesus in the temple courts, using a key term for praise, "Hosanna!"). And the word for "infants" refers to a newborn child at his or her mother's breast – those whose babblings are both praise and strength. The religious elitists know all these nuances well.

Second, Jesus says in John 3:17 that he comes into the world not to condemn, but to save. Condemnation is self-pronounced, and as augmented by the "accuser," a name for the devil. Thus, Jesus allows this self-condemnation by his enemies to understatedly manifest. Namely, the chief priests and teachers of the law repeat the rest of the sentence from Psalm 8:2 in their minds, "because of your enemies, to silence the foe and the avenger." It is unspoken, and they can either publicly distance themselves from identifying with these words, or they can act in accordance with them, showing by their opposition to Jesus that he is the Messiah and they are his self-chosen enemies.

They are trapped in their own hypocrisies, and more furious in their souls than ever. They know that Jesus knows that they know what is happening – exactly. And the majority of the onlookers sense it too. Incredible and true theater at the epicenter of the contest of the ages. Jesus gets them to diagnose their own status, thus making his judgments certain in their own eyes.

Third, we now arrive at what is really happening. At the deeper level, the chief priests and teachers of the law are telling Jesus to shut up the children's praise, and to stop all this political talk about him being the Son of David. In response, Jesus is giving an unmistakable message, which we can paraphrase this way: "Not only will I not shut them up, but their praise, which you despise as weakness, is actually my strength. You are the foes of the Messiah, I am the Messiah and their praise will silence you instead. Any further questions gentlemen?"

Explosive.

And fourth, there is another sub-textual element that ratchets up the challenge. The chief priests want to disprove Jesus as the Messiah, to show him failing to fulfill the Messianic prophecies thus far quoted. But they have yet to succeed. Jesus knows this, so in his sub-textual challenge, in the spirit of his precise sarcasm, we can imagine these words: "Gentlemen, all you have to do to prove that I am not the Messiah is to keep on babbling like babies, to keep on talking. For, if you are able, you can disprove the eighth psalm and show that you are not the enemies of the true Messiah." But to babble like an infant is to embrace the "weakness" they despise. They create a trap for themselves that Jesus identifies.

As well, we noted earlier that the chief priests introduce a sub-textual innuendo that Jesus is no better than the lifeless pagan god Ba'al, in the question of whether or not he hears what the children were saying. Here Jesus answers that innuendo as he quotes the biblical language of Psalm 8, literally, "children and suckling babes."

In other words, some of these children are so young that they cannot speak articulately, but only babble. The children who shout "Hosanna to the Son of David" are older and articulate, yet they are regarded by the chief priests as weak and despised. So Jesus, in quoting Psalm 8, takes some "babbling" children, weaker and more despised yet by the elitists, and uses them as an example of his true strength in the face of their pretense.

In using the term "babble," we are gleaning a sub-textual reality that refers to the Tower of Babel (from which we trace the verb, "to babble"), in its confusion of languages and nations. Jesus is hinting at a double entendre – babbling is the strength of little children, but folly for adults. "Babbling" adults trace back to the original source of paganism and polity that challenges Yahweh Elohim – Babylonian religion. Jesus thus hints: "Who and what, gentlemen, are truly pagan?" This debate between Jesus and his enemies is truly the contest of the ages.

Then, to conclude: "If you do not silence yourselves you triumph."

What a simple offer, and yet the nuances were many, for all they have to do is babble like a newborn or toddler – they do not have to be cogent or truthful, they just have to resist being silenced by the strength of childlikeness. Shrewdness and innocence joined, balance struck. And how they hate such an analogy, given their mockery of the children. They seek to dig a pit for Jesus, but they themselves fall into it.

Essentially, Jesus gives them an offer they cannot refuse – a level playing field with the most gracious terms possible. Jesus will be teaching in the Court of the Gentiles during Passover week to the throngs, they are invited to attend, and they only have to maintain the power of a filibuster.

The debate is set.

Their chosen descent into hell, into their own trap, is gathering force.

They are free to step out of their trap anytime, but they love their idols of the temple, political power and money more than truth and mercy.

Chapter Six

Strike One: Credentials

Intensity

The eyeball-to-eyeball intensity between Jesus and his enemies must have been remarkable for the onlookers to witness – especially for the blind who have just been healed. His authority is unmatched, and it is Good News for all those seeking release from the false arrangement between the religious elitists and the occupying Roman Empire. They are watching their Messiah in action as the Deliverer, and they can judge the soul of Jesus, out of whom the Light shines, versus the souls of the religious elitists, into whom the darkness retreats.

When the chief priests and the teachers of the law challenge Jesus, it is important to note that they do not challenge him on the "facts" of the case. They do not challenge his reason to overturn the tables of the money changers, or the benches of those selling doves, or the rightness of it, and they do not challenge his healings as faked or inappropriate (and it is not the Sabbath, so their singular excuse to challenge him here is not available).

They know they cannot challenge these facts, so they try another route to discredit him. They try to take the focus away from the theme of the Son of David, especially as professed by the children.

They flee to secondary questions because they cannot deal with the primary reality. Secondary questions are valid, and must be answered, but unless the primary facts are discussed, there is no embrace of honest communication.

By their inability to challenge the primary realities of Jesus – as the Son of David, with authority to judge the hypocrites and heal the sick – his enemies know they are stuck. So they come up with secondary questions in the hope of tripping Jesus up, to remove any focus on the primary facts of the case. In an honest court of law, unless there is agreement as to the facts, no judgment can be rendered. But the religious lawyers who oppose Jesus are not in service to true law.

As Jesus answers their indignant question about "hearing" the children, honestly turning the tables on them, he makes a powerfully implicit invitation for them to keep on speaking and challenging him. But their immediate response is silence. Psalm 8 is being initially fulfilled.

But Jesus is patient, wanting them to have the fullest considered opportunity not to be silenced. He hopes they too will join the praise and be saved from their evil ways. He is offering them a level playing field to make their best case. But they merely stand there with nothing to say as six Messianic prophecies have been fulfilled so far in their presence, despite their best efforts. So Jesus lets them plot their next move, he is in complete control, and leave the city to spend the night in the neighboring town of Bethany.

Credentials

The next morning as Jesus and his disciples are heading back to the city, he curses a fig tree with leaves on it, but without the fruit it should have had (Matthew 21:18-22). This is understood to be another act of judgment, for the fig tree is a symbol for the nation Israel. Earlier and repeatedly Jesus has chastised those among his fellow Jews who refuse to recognize the season of the Messiah's appearance. The disciples are amazed at how quickly the tree withers, and Jesus uses this moment to teach them about a faith that can remove mountains. In other words, no matter how accursed the theological or political state of affairs might be – and they are in the midst of such accursedness – the power to overcome such evil is given to believers.

When Jesus speaks of "this mountain," he is standing opposite Mount Zion, which is also a name for Jerusalem as the City of David. The city with its imposing temple is the obvious visual reference point for the disciples. Also, Jesus is making reference to one of the most dominating Messianic prophecies in the Tanakh, the entirety of Psalm 2, where in v. 6 the Lord declares, "I have installed my King on Zion, my holy hill." Thus, we see a seventh Messianic prophecy, implicitly, for the readers of Matthew's gospel to consider here.

Here we have the Son of David prophesying that just as the fig tree, a symbol of the nation, is judged and destroyed since it pretends to produce fruit it does not, so too with the City of David. This is because, along with the temple, it has become an idol to the elitists. This theme of the coming judgment on Jerusalem permeates Passover week in the first coming of Jesus, and also as the new Jerusalem is provided for in his second coming.

Jesus is coming back to the Court of the Gentiles in his proactive purpose to teach the people, knowing too that he has set the table for the debate with his enemies. Matthew 21:23-27 reads:

> Jesus entered the temple courts, and, while he was teaching, the chief priests and the elders of the people came to him. "By what authority are you doing these things?" they asked. "And who gave you this authority?"
>
> Jesus replied, "I will also ask you one question. If you answer me, I will tell you by what authority I am doing these things. John's baptism – where did it come from? Was it from heaven, or from men?"
>
> They discussed it among themselves and said, "If we say, 'From heaven,' he will ask, 'Then why didn't you believe him?' But if we say, 'From men' – we are afraid of the people, for they all hold that John was a prophet."
>
> So they answered Jesus, "We don't know."
>
> Then he said, "Neither will I tell you by what authority I am doing these things" (cf. Mark 11:27-33; Luke 20:1-8).

Since they cannot challenge his deeds, they try to challenge his "authority" or "credentials," based on their elitist assumptions. Jesus has not studied in one of their rabbinic schools in Jerusalem, nor sat at the feet of one of their teachers. So they seek to dismiss him as ignorant and unqualified to judge sin, teach the people and heal their infirmities. Jesus meets them head on, not by playing to their elitist perspective, but by treating them as elites.

To be an "elite" is good, if the privileges of the education and resources that come with it are employed to honor the power to give blessings to others. "Elitism" is when the privileges are used for the power to take from others, to curse them. Since the chief priests are given their religious authority by means of an elite education, Jesus challenges them to live up to the ability of true elites. He is giving them a level playing field. Or, as it were, making paraphrase: "If you ask me a leading question, fine. But first show me the integrity of answering my leading question, and then I will know if you are truly elite, able to take in what you dish out."

The situation is almost comical. There are thousands of people listening to Jesus. We can imagine the chief priests and the elders huddling together like a football team, deciding their next play. But while in their huddle, the fans are not in the stands, but on the field, adjacent with bended ear, and it is home turf for the Messiah.

The religious elitists have two options.

Option "A" is to admit the truth – that John the Baptist received his authority from heaven.

There are undoubtedly some Pharisees in this group who went to watch the people being baptized by John, only to have been rebuked for their hypocrisies (see Matthew 3:7-10). They know John's authority, but because he threatened their elitist stature, they were sure not going to submit to it. They know that John testifies to Jesus as the Messiah, and to accept John's authority as heavenly means they have to also believe in Jesus – the one thing they are firmly in opposition to doing. So option "A" has to be scratched – they cannot admit the truth because they will not submit to it.

Option "B" is to market a lie – that John the Baptist received his authority from human imagination.

But here the text reveals a moment of candor. The "elders of the people" are afraid of the people (cf. Mark 11:32), which reinforces the reality of their elitist stature. The chief priests and the elders also have to scratch option "B," because they know the people hold John to be a prophet.

In the accounts of Passover week by Mark and Luke, we see additional elements of the agenda of the religious elitists, and their fears. After Jesus cleanses the Court of the Gentiles of the sellers and money changers, and before their question about the authority of Jesus, the text in Luke reads: "Every day he was teaching at the temple. But the chief priests, the teachers of the law and the leaders among the people were trying to kill him. Yet they could not find any way to do it, because all the people hung on his words" (19:47-48; cf. Mark 11:18).

Then in the account of their response to Jesus' question about John the Baptist, Luke puts option "B" this way: "But if we say, 'From men,' all the people will stone us, because they are persuaded that John was a prophet" (20:6). So their fears are tangible – their very lives were on the line.

Pretension of Ignorance

Thus, they have to choose option "C," the pretension of ignorance.

The people are overwhelmingly on Jesus' side, and the religious elitists are an island of insecurity in their midst, with enough pretense to think they rule over the people, but deathly afraid of rousing their opposition. They know if they challenge the credentials of John the Baptist, they will be stoned to death on the spot. As they consider this option, we can imagine one of the elitist squad looking over his shoulder at the crowd of people and feeling the intensity of their gaze. The pretense of ignorance is the only way out of their dilemma if they want to keep alive and keep their positions intact.

They do not have a) the courage to admit the truth, or b) the temerity to lie and face the public sentiment. This is Jesus' domain – open public debate on a level playing field. So they cowardly choose option "C" to pretend to be ignorant, the "we don't know" position. It follows in the footsteps of Cain, giving us a battle between the sons of Cain and the Son of David. Genesis 4:8-12 reads:

Now Cain said to his brother Abel, "Let's go out to the field." And while they were in the field, Cain attacked his brother Abel and killed him.

Then the LORD said to Cain, "Where is your brother Abel?"

"I don't know," he replied. "Am I my brother's keeper?"

The LORD said, "What have you done? Listen! Your brother's blood cries out to me from the ground. Now you are under a curse and driven from the ground, which opened its mouth to receive your brother's blood from your hand. When you work the ground, it will no longer yield its crops for you. You will be a restless wanderer on the earth."

As it has been said, you can fool some of the people all of the time, and all the people some of the time, but not all the people all the time (and especially, you can't fool Mom). This is completely the case with Yahweh Elohim – he who is greater than space, time and number in the very essence of his name. Cain does not have a) the courage to admit the truth that he killed his brother, because he is not going to repent; and he does not have b) the audacity or folly to lie and tell Yahweh that Abel is somewhere else. He knows God knows the truth. Thus Cain becomes testy as he is caught in the lie, and he makes the cowardly choice c) to plead ignorance, the "I don't know" argument. Then he challenges God, "Am I my brother's keeper?" His guilt is advertised in his very rhetorical question, as he is in fact his brother's killer, not the keeper he should have been.

The "I don't know" argument is the weakest possible form of moral argument in human history.

It is employed when the truth cannot be admitted because accountability will come into place, and when the lie cannot be successfully marketed. When a genuine ignorance is in place, there is the possibility of openness to truth, of a willingness to change. But with Cain and the Pharisees, their responses to the light of the questions, is to flee into the darkness. No openness to the truth, no willingness to change. Their "I don't know" arguments are excuses to justify murder, ex post facto for Abel, and in the trajectory of the elitist agenda for Jesus.

In Matthew's gospel, he has the very mimic of Cain's "I don't know" argument in view. All the same idolatry is in place, the murderous intents and opposition to the Messianic lineage. Yet Jesus loves them and is patient with them, speaking the truth in love. When he is challenged by their hypocrisy, Jesus responds by creating a level playing field. He gives them opportunity to show whether their position holds any integrity, and when they fail to show it, they are the ones who condemn themselves, not Jesus. And yet, the invitation to repentance is always on the table, so long as the enemies of Jesus still have the breath of life.

Thus, Jesus treats his enemies with respect. Since they will not rise to a level playing field, Jesus will not demean them by answering their question. He is calling them to a higher standard than they expect of themselves, he is calling them to be who they should be in their leadership roles. He treats the chief priests as the highest echelon of the teachers of the law, and the rabbis and the elders of the people likewise with respect.

This he does in the classical rabbinic style of answering a question with a question to probe for truth and the satisfaction of honest learning. In so doing, Jesus defines the terms of the debate. In order for there to be informed choice and the pursuit of truth, terms must be accurately defined, and accurate definitions cannot be reached without honest communication. His enemies refuse the communication, so Jesus holds out, not allowing their inaccurate terms, their pretensions of ignorance, to become accepted in public dialogue.

Jesus continues his response in v. 28 by saying "What do you think?" From here he gives three parables – of the two sons, the tenants and the wedding banquet (Matthew 21:28-22:14). In each parable his focus is on who will inherit God's kingdom, and in each case it is "a people who will produce its fruit," such people as tax collectors (i.e., "traitors") and prostitutes who repent, and not the elitists who view it as their privileged domain. In the second parable, the eighth Messianic prophecy in this debate is referenced, again from Psalm 118 (which is also quoted in a different section by the people in his triumphal entry). Here, Jesus challenges his enemies the way he does in first turning the tables on them:

Jesus said to them, "Have you never read in the Scriptures:

" 'The stone the builders rejected
    has become the capstone;
the Lord has done this,
    and it is marvelous in our eyes'?

"Therefore I tell you that the kingdom of God will be taken away from you and given to a people who will produce its fruit. He who falls on this stone will be broken to pieces, but he on whom it falls will be crushed."

When the chief priests and the Pharisees heard Jesus' parables, they knew he was talking about them. They looked for a way to arrest him, but they were afraid of the crowd because the people held that he was a prophet (21:42-46).

In the first parable, the chief priests and the Pharisees understand they are being told they are like the second son who says he would obey his father, but does not. But the "tax collectors and the prostitutes are entering the kingdom of God ahead of you" (v. 31), for they are like the first son who initially disobeys his father, then changes his mind and obeys. In the second parable, Jesus identifies them as the killers of the vineyard owner's son, and then quotes Psalm 118 that shows them to be those who reject the "capstone," the Messiah.

The religious elitists are the enemies, the foes and avengers who are to be silenced. But they still do not, will not, get it. Jesus is in full control. These religious elitists, well educated and proud, are silenced in Jesus' presence as they refuse to engage him on a level playing field. In the wake of the first two parables, they do not engage Jesus, but they again huddle among themselves, surrounded by a crowd of people they fear. Jesus then continues with his third parable concerning the wedding banquet, where the same themes are reiterated – their rejection of the kingdom of God, and the acceptance by the needy.

The encounter with Psalm 8 leads the chief priests and elders to challenge the authority and credentials of Jesus. They are followed by their co-belligerent peers, in what ultimately proves to be a four-fold attempt to trip up Jesus with secondary questions. The enemies of Jesus continued to be self-silenced.

Strike one.

Chapter Seven

Strike Two: Church and State

So now, the second formal attempt is made in Matthew 22:15-22:

> Then the Pharisees went out and laid plans to trap him in his words. They sent their disciples to him along with the Herodians.

> "Teacher," they said, "we know you are a man of integrity and that you teach the way of God in accordance with the truth. You aren't swayed by men, because you pay no attention to who they are. Tell us then, what is your opinion? Is it right to pay taxes to Caesar or not?"

> But Jesus, knowing their evil intent, said, "You hypocrites, why are you trying to trap me? Show me the coin used for paying the tax." They brought him a denarius, and he asked them, "Whose portrait is this? And whose inscription?"

> "Caesar's," they replied. Then he said to them, "Give to Caesar what is Caesar's, and to God what is God's."

> When they heard this, they were amazed. So they left him and went away.

They are unable to trap him in what he says, and astonished by his answer, they become silent.

The Pharisees are theologically orthodox, calculating nationalists, even agitators, opposed to the Roman occupation, and waiting for the right moment to see the Roman yoke cast off. Part of that calculation is their toleration of working with Rome and Herod in the meantime, insofar as necessary.

The Herodians are an eclectic lot, and they support the rule of the Herods in preference to direct rule by Roman prefects. Some of them may be Sadducees (whom we will meet shortly), who deeply oppose the Pharisees on theological terms. But their primary identity here is political. So the Herodians oppose the Pharisees and are opposed by the Pharisees.

But though the Pharisees and Herodians hate each other, they hate Jesus more. So they conspire against him. From the ancient Near East there is a proverb: "The enemy of my enemy is my friend." (At least until the mutual enemy is destroyed, after which newfound friends return to their old ways and become each other's enemies once again.)

Because of a mutual fear of Jesus, perceived as a threat to both of their elitist positions the Pharisees and Herodians put aside their mutual distrust for the moment, and conspire to entrap Jesus. They figure they can get him from both sides at once. From the Pharisaical perspective, the question of credentials did not work, so now they devise a plan to pose what has become the classic "church and state" question – Christ versus Caesar.

Thus the Pharisees send some of their disciples along with the hated Herodians. This reveals their insecurity, for having already been directly silenced, the Pharisees now shield their egos with proxies.

These Pharisaical disciples begin with flattery. They know, and Jesus knows that they know, and the people in the Court of the Gentiles know they and the Herodians know it is an inept attempt at flattery for the sake of an ulterior agenda. Yet when the best argument they can make is an "I don't know" posture, moral ineptitude only gathers speed in its downward spiral, as sin is unrelinquished. We can imagine their spokesman clearing his throat and attempting to sound sincere, knowing the whole while his ruse. The irony is that the Pharisees would not choose option "A" in response to Jesus' question about the authority of John the Baptist. They would not admit the truth then, but now their disciples say Jesus teaches the truth.

It is tragicomedy throughout, and magnified when they then say to Jesus: "You aren't swayed by men, because you pay no attention to who they are." They are condemning their own Pharisaical party. They are admitting that truth tellers are not impressed or influenced by social elitists. And at the same time they are frustrated with Jesus, because in the first formal question, the Pharisees tried to intimidate him by their claim to social position. They have the official credentials and Jesus does not. But he is unimpressed with them, and their egos are crushed. The Pharisees are the men who cannot sway Jesus, and neither can their disciples.

Now we have the second attempt at a secondary question. The Pharisaical disciples ask his opinion about paying taxes to Caesar. Their hope is that either answer Jesus gives, yes or no, will be his undoing.

If Jesus said yes to paying taxes to Caesar, then the Pharisees can hold him up as a traitor to the nation. Surely, in their view, the Messiah would be an immediate political figure, overthrowing Caesar, and would in no way pay taxes to the one he came to overthrow. There is hypocrisy in this since the Pharisees have to pay taxes to hold their position, but they are willing to risk it in their desperation to prove Jesus not to be the Messiah. But specially, they want to accuse Jesus of idolatry.

The denarius coin has a portrait of Tiberius Caesar on it, and on the reverse side it reads in Latin: "Tiberius Caesar, son of the divine Augustus." It is a claim to deity by the son of a false deity, to which the true Son of God is a direct threat. The Pharisees can rationalize that the handling of this money is the pollution of idolatry, and surely no Messiah would handle it. They think that if Jesus says yes to the payment of taxes, they could then accuse him of regarding Caesar as a god, accuse him of idolatry and discredit him in front of the people.

If Jesus said no to paying the taxes, the Herodians could accuse him of political insurrection and treason against Herod and/or Rome (a little duplicity here), and have him crucified accordingly.

These co-belligerents have Jesus trapped, regardless of what he says, so they think.

At this point, in round two, Jesus calls a spade a spade – he sees their "evil intent" and "duplicity" and calls them hypocrites, as is evident to all present. He only does so because they have already admitted it to his face – refusing one moment to admit the truth (in round one), and having their disciples flatter him as a truth teller the next (in round two).

Jesus does not initiate the need to call a spade a spade. He only gives response to blatant hypocrisy. The Son of God comes not to condemn, but to save. Those who are condemned are those who refuse to live in the light because they know their deeds are evil – they are self-condemned in their choice not to believe in God's one and only Son (see John 3:17-21). Jesus is the Light, and he only diagnoses the darkness after it diagnoses itself.

Yet with such a diagnosis, Jesus still treats them with respect, giving them opportunity once again to measure up to the truth. He gives them a level playing field. With his words exposing their entrapping intent, he appeals to a definition of terms, to an examination of the facts at hand. To put it another way: "Show me the coin, show me the evidence in question and let's look at it together." So a denarius is brought, and Jesus asks a question of obvious certainty to all involved. Facts are facts, and are always in service to the truth of the Gospel. "Whose portrait and inscription is on the coin?" They answer, and in so doing, are morally cornered into owning the answer. It is Caesar's portrait. "Then give Caesar what is Caesar's, and give God what is God's."

They stand there dumbfounded and amazed, astonished and silent, jaws open and nothing to say. Silenced a second time, and they have no strategy for a comeback. Whereas the Pharisees and Herodians conspire to trap Jesus in their idolatry of political power, he specifically calls them to consider the image of God.

The moment he says "portrait" and "inscription," the Jewish mind immediately goes back to Genesis 1:26-28 and the foundation of the "image" and "likeness" of God.

We are God's portrait. We are the finite image-bearers of the infinite Creator, endowed with the stewardship to rule over his good creation.

These proxy Pharisees, students having already memorized the entire Hebrew Bible, immediately know what Jesus is saying. And along with the Herodians, they know he is challenging their actual idolatry of the temple and political power. And Jesus has already answered the Pharisees earlier, in reference to himself, "I tell you that one greater than the temple is here" (Matthew 12:6).

Namely, to expand and paraphrase Jesus' words to the Pharisaical party: "If Caesar is so foolish to call himself a god and circulate a coin that says so, then give him back his portrait and folly. There is no fear in touching a coin of idolatry, since idols are nothing. Let's see what comes of his claim when he stands before the true God on Judgment Day. If Ba'al is god, let him contend for himself. If Caesar is a god, let him contend for himself. In the meantime, it is no loss for a true worshiper of God to pay taxes. But most importantly, give God back his portrait – which is not our money inscribed with the name of a pretender, but our souls, which are made in God's image and are his true possession."

In the order of creation, man and woman are made in God's image to rule over the creation, and Jesus is coming to restore that true rule in face of the false rule.

To the Herodians, says Jesus, again in paraphrase to help us imagine the deeper realities at play: "God is not interested in your money and politics, and its attendant idolatry. He does not want Caesar or Herod's image, or that of anyone or anything else. He wants you, the image-bearers of God; he wants your heart, soul, mind and strength. Nothing less."

This is indeed the most powerful statement of conflict between church and state in history. This is a contest between Caesar, who is a pretender, son of a false god, and Jesus, the true Son of the living God. This is a context between a false messiah and the true Messiah. Whom shall we serve? Jesus is calling both the Pharisees and Herodians to give their wills to God, to repent and confess him as the Messiah.

Their temporal political agendas are no match for his eternal political agenda – the kingdom of Satan and human ego versus the kingdom of God. And they know it. They think they have devised a conflict between temple and state in which Jesus would become mired, but Jesus shows that for the true believer there is no conflict. Our citizenship in the eternal kingdom of

God defines for us our temporal citizenship. The enemies of Jesus again silence themselves.

Strike two.

Chapter Eight

Strike Three: Theological Nitpicking

Matthew's text continues in 22:23-33 with the third attempt to derail Jesus with a secondary question:

> That same day the Sadducees, who say there is no resurrection, came to him with a question. "Teacher," they said, "Moses told us that if a man dies without having children, his brother must marry the widow and have children for him. Now there were seven brothers among us. The first one married and died, and since he had no children, he left his wife to his brother. The same thing happened to the second and third brother, right on down to the seventh. Finally, the woman died. Now then, at the resurrection, whose wife will she be of the seven, since all of them were married to her?"

> Jesus replied, "You are in error because you do not know the Scriptures or the power of God. At the resurrection people will neither marry nor be given in marriage; they will be like the angels in heaven. But about the resurrection of the dead – have you not read what God said to you, 'I am the God of Abraham, the God of Isaac, and the God of Jacob'? He is not the God of the dead but of the living."

> When the crowds heard this, they were astonished at his teaching (cf. Mark 12:18-27; Luke 20:27-39).

The Sadducees are the wealthiest and most culturally refined of the religious elitists, and also the smallest in number. In proper terms they are heretics, because they deny the resurrection and the existence of angels. To deny the resurrection is to deny the tree of life that God originally gives Adam in the Garden of Eden, and its final restoration.

Thus it denies the biblical foundation of creation, sin and redemption as rooted in Genesis 1-3. To deny the existence of angels is to deny the historical testimony and reliability of the Hebrew Bible in its many and consistent references to the ministry of angels and their key role as God's messengers to the covenant people of the Messianic lineage.

Yet though they are heretics, and Jesus dispatches with their error, his greater concern in the gospels is with the Pharisees, who are theologically orthodox. They believe the Tanakh is fully inspired by God, including its definition of the ministry of angels and the promise of the resurrection.

There is a greater danger posed by the theologically orthodox who are hypocrites, than by the heretics who are hypocrites.

As the Pharisees and Herodians are silenced by Jesus, the Sadducees see their opportunity, with a theological agenda in the forefront. They figure if they can silence Jesus, then they will be at the top of the heap in terms of theology, in contrast to the Pharisees; and they will separate themselves from those among their fellow Sadducees who are politically motivated Herodians.

The Sadducees are seeking to assert superiority in handling the Scriptures, and in a nitpicking fashion. Thus, to understand both their agendas, and Jesus' response, we need to know the background issues at play.

The reference point they begin with is Moses' words in Deuteronomy 25:5-6:

> If brothers are living together and one of them dies without a son, his
> widow must not marry outside the family. Her husband's
> brother shall take her and marry her and fulfill the duty of a
> brother-in-law to her. The first son she bears shall carry on the
> name of the dead brother so that his name will not be blotted out
> from Israel.

This scenario defines what is known as "levirate" (brother-in-law) marriage, and part of a larger definition of the "kinsmen-redeemer" law. It envisions an unmarried brother living in the same household with his brother and wife (as opposed to already having his own household as a married man), on land they both inherited from their father.

The Law of Moses holds in high regard the name and inheritance of all the Israelites, where the land is to stay in each family line throughout the years. This way there can be no centralization of top-down political power gained by amassing land. This is why the year of Jubilee is instituted in Leviticus 25, intended so that all land would be returned to its family lineage at least every 50 years. Samuel as judge presides over a locally based and decentralized definition of power (see 1 Samuel 7:15-17), and this is why he is so grieved when Israel clamors for a king like the pagan nations (see 1 Samuel 8:1-21). Saul, as such a king, then presides over a top-down enslaving government.

Limited and locally based government, not top-down government, is the biblical motif.

In such a Hebrew community ethic, a childless widow could keep the land in the name of her late husband by the graciousness of her brother-in-law. She has already left her father and mother and their land, joining her husband's inheritance. The first son would take on her first husband's name and inheritance in legal terms, with the second son receiving the birthright of her second husband, and biological father of both. It is the power to give, where social cohesion, prosperity and individual identity are well balanced.

And the brother-in-law is normally glad to do so. He loses nothing, for he still rears his first biological son, and he gains the continuity of his late brother's name, indeed of their mutual family name tracing back to their own father.

In Genesis 38, Onan refuses to honor his late brother Er in levirate marriage to Tamar, and is judged accordingly. In the book of Ruth, when Ruth the Moabitess returns to Israel, recently widowed and with her widowed mother-in-law Naomi, it is this same kinsman-redeemer law that leads to her marriage to Boaz. She thus becomes the great-grandmother of David, and hence a foremother to the Son of David.

The Sadducees know all this, and draw on a rich tradition when they refer to the kinsman-redeemer law. But their purpose is not the love of hard questions; it is ulterior. The people can see the strained attempt on the part of the Sadducees – seven men in a row dying and leaving the same woman childless. In the apocryphal book of Tobit, there is a story told of a woman named Sarah who was "given in marriage to seven husbands, and before the marriage could be regularly consummated they had all been killed by the wicked demon Asmodaeus" (3:8, New English Bible). The Sadducees know this tale, they know it is apocryphal and not regarded as part of the Hebrew Bible in any portion of Jewish history. It is nonetheless suitable for their purposes, as they are not orthodox to begin with.

Even still, though a secondary question to the real issue, phrased in the extreme, it deserves an answer, which Jesus provides. But it also highlights the moral bankruptcy of those who live in the darkness. They are grasping at straws, having ranged far afield of the original question in their desperate attempt to hold on to false power, as true power advances into their midst.

In his answer, Jesus is blunt – the Sadducees know neither the Scriptures, nor the power of God. Mark includes Jesus' more stinging words at the end, "You are badly mistaken!" (12:27), and Luke includes Jesus' invitation to faith, "... for to him all are alive" (20:38).

The Sadducees know the Scriptures, so they think, but they do not know the power of the Scriptures, and of God's presence. Since they reject the interpretive basis of the order of creation, they also forfeit the tree of life in the Garden of Eden, and its nature that precedes and provides the expectation of the resurrection. They will not, cannot understand it.

So Jesus speaks to them in terms they can understand. In referring to the God of Abraham, Isaac and Jacob, he says that these words of God are addressed to them as their descendants too. This the Sadducees wish to believe to begin with.

Now we have need for a brief detour into some technical language. This will greatly help us understand the power of Jesus' response – to help us get inside the storyline of the text where there is the need to unpack the theological nitpicking at play.

When Jesus uses the present tense "I am the God" (*ego eimi ho theos*), he is quoting Yahweh's appearance to Moses in the burning bush in Exodus 3:6 (which in the Septuagint is *ego eimi ho on*, "I am the One"). This is virtually the language in John 8:58 (*ego eimi*), used thirty-one times in John's gospel, when Jesus equates his person with the name of *Yahweh* ("I AM") – as Exodus 3:14 calls *Yahweh* the "I AM" *(ego eimi* in the Septuagint).

The Sadducees want, so they think, the I AM of God – Yahweh Elohim who is the divine Eternal Presence. When Jesus gives them his Presence as the incarnate I AM, and follows through with the simple conclusion that God is the God not of the dead but of the living, the whole power of the I AM that transcends space, time and number hits them with full force.

They are speechless. They cannot reduce God to a space-time-number bound pagan deity. And if Yahweh is the present tense God of Abraham, Isaac and Jacob – the very forefathers to whom they claim allegiance – and if he is speaking also to them in the present, then the Sadducees cannot object to the resurrection without a) saying God is a god of the dead, and/or b) that they themselves are dead people. God is the God of Abraham, Isaac and Jacob – present tense – because they are alive in God's presence awaiting the final resurrection of all the saints. Jesus knows the Scriptures and the power of God, and the Sadducees know they cannot dispute his knowledge.

In essence, the Sadducees are involved in a matter of theological nitpicking, but also, completely unprepared for Jesus' dexterity in handling it. Jesus answers their ulterior question by rooting it in the deeper reality of the Scriptures, and the crowds are astonished. The Sadducees have nothing more to say, except that Jesus gives his enemies as many opportunities to ask him questions or give their perspectives as they wish.

Strike three.

Chapter Nine

Strike Four: Theological Grandstanding

The storyline continues in 22:34-46 with the fourth and final valid, but diversionary, question:

> Hearing that Jesus had silenced the Sadducees, the Pharisees got together. One of them, an expert in the law, tested him with this question: "Teacher, which is the greatest commandment in the Law?"

> Jesus replied: " 'Love the Lord your God with all your heart and with all your soul and with all your mind.' This is the first and greatest commandment. And the second is like it: 'Love your neighbor as yourself.' All the Law and the Prophets hang on these two commandments."

> While the Pharisees were gathered together, Jesus asked them, "What do you think about the Christ? Whose son is he?"

> "The son of David," they replied.

> He said to them, "How is it then that David, speaking by the Spirit, calls him 'Lord'? For he says,

> " 'The Lord said to my Lord:
>   "Sit at my right hand
> until I put your enemies
>   under your feet." '

> "If then David calls him 'Lord,' how can he be his son?" No one could say a word in reply, and from that day on no one dared to ask him any more questions.

In Mark's gospel, he organizes the material of this encounter somewhat differently, with the addition of identifying the man who asks the question. We read in 12:28-34:

> One of the teachers of the law came and heard them debating. Noticing that Jesus had given them a good answer, he asked him, "Of all the commandments, which is the most important?"

> "The most important one," answered Jesus, "is this: 'Hear, O Israel, the Lord our God, the Lord is one. Love the Lord your God with all your heart and with all your soul and with all your mind and with all your strength.' The second is this: 'Love your neighbor as yourself.' There is no commandment greater than these."

> "Well said, teacher," the man replied. "You are right in saying that God is one and there is no other but him. To love him with all your heart, with all your understanding and with all your strength, and to love your neighbor as yourself is more important than all burnt offerings and sacrifices."

> When Jesus saw that he had answered wisely, he said to him, "You are not far from the kingdom of God." And from then on no one dared ask him any more questions.

The enemies of Jesus are being whittled down to the point of self-censorship where they fear asking Jesus any more questions.

When the Pharisees see that the Sadducees have been silenced, Matthew focuses on their desire to come back again at Jesus to try and silence him. Thus Matthew reports that "one of them, an expert in the law" poses the final question. He does not identify who the man is, or the motivation of his question, only that the Pharisees who have been debating Jesus want to see this question succeed in silencing Jesus.

Mark shows the specific motivation of the man asking the question, identifying him, not as one of the group of Pharisees who have been debating that week with Jesus, but another Pharisee, "one of the teachers of the law," who comes to hear the debate and now joins in, seeing how wisely Jesus has answered the Sadducees. This teacher of the law is seeking the truth ("Baruch" in Book One). He asks his genuine question about the central truth of the Law, and the other Pharisees become parasites on the back of his question, with the opposite hope. They have been silenced twice before, and are out of material to try and trap Jesus in his words. Thus they jump on this question, and Matthew portrays their angle.

When this honest Pharisee says that loving God and neighbor is more important than all burnt offerings and sacrifices, he is affirming Jesus' teaching of the Law.

He quotes the substance of these words back to Jesus in the temple courts. Jesus knows well his words to the Pharisees recorded both in Matthew 9:13, "But go and learn what this means: 'I desire mercy, not sacrifice,' " and in 12:7, "If you had known what these words mean, 'I desire mercy, not sacrifice' " (as we addressed in the Introduction).

This honest Pharisee likely heard these words, whether firsthand or by the report of the other Pharisees, and undoubtedly knows and/or went and truly learns what Jesus means by them. Thus, Jesus says that this man is not far from the kingdom of God. All that lacks, we might suppose, is a final confession of Jesus as the Messiah, and the willingness to thus forsake the elitisms of his position and serve as a true elite, a true teacher of the Law.

As this fourth and final round of debate moves toward conclusion, the Greek grammar yields an additional element in comparison with the NIV, reading in Matthew 22:41: "While the Pharisees were *still* gathered together, Jesus asked them ..." In other words, they are still standing there with nothing more to say.

Jesus answers their fourth secondary question, one of theological centrality from the perspective of the honest Pharisee, one of theological grandstanding in terms of the dishonest Pharisees and their agenda.

Also, Jesus is cementing his answer to the question by the Pharisees and Herodians on paying taxes to Caesar, as it were: "He wants you, the image-bearers of God; he wants your heart, soul, mind and strength. Nothing less."

Strike four.

In seeking to avoid the Son of David question where they have been stymied, the enemies of Jesus invested in four chosen angles to trip Jesus up. None of them worked, and they thus ran out of options:

1. Challenging Jesus on his authority and credentials.
2. Challenging Jesus on the separation of temple and state.
3. Challenging Jesus on an issue of theological nitpicking.
4. Challenging Jesus on an issue of theological grandstanding.

Chapter Ten

Back to Square One

The Son of David

So Jesus stands there (in humble confidence), and the Pharisees stand there (in exposed hypocrisy, silenced), and the large crowds stand there (in eager anticipation of what will happen next), and the honest teacher of the law, perhaps with some of his honest peers, stands there (likewise in eager anticipation).

Jesus gives his enemies the freedom to test him at every level, and he knows that they know, as the crowds know, that they are at the dead end of their intellectual, moral and spiritual ability to invent new arguments, at least in public assembly. (They do invent another pretense after Jesus is arrested, but in secret assembly.) Jesus allows his enemies to take the issue away from its true focus, from the primary question to secondary ones, and now that their agenda is exhausted, Jesus is free to return the debate to its point of origin, and to the real issue at stake.

There is no disputing the facts of Jesus' moral and supernatural authority in overturning the tables of the money changers and benches of those selling doves, and in the healing of the blind and lame. The question goes back to the objections of the chief priests, and the teachers of the law, to the crowds and children calling Jesus the "Son of David," the Messiah, the Christ. They have tried to have him silence this proclamation. So Jesus challenges their right to silence the children's Messianic praises of him, and he engages them in a contest of silencings, rooted in the quote from Psalm 8.

Thus, Jesus returns to square one, and since the religious elitists have objected to his being called the Son of David, he asks them the positive question about their views of the coming Christ – whose son is he? This is a simple question to which he knows that they know the answer – a simple point of fact. We can imagine some of the Pharisees thinking to themselves, or perhaps even verbalizing to Jesus a fuller response: "Why, the Son of David! Why do you think we are so upset with you? You have allowed yourself to be called the Messiah, who is the true Son of David, and we know that you're not (though we can't prove it yet)!"

Jesus is in control of the language and ethics of the debate, above reproach in all he does. Thus he appeals to an authority that even his enemies cannot dispute – he cites the Holy Spirit speaking through David in the words of Psalm 110, another Messianic psalm, the ninth Messianic prophecy being fulfilled in this debate.

So the Pharisees give the right answer, and Jesus agrees with them. But then follows the question that exposes their dishonesty, paraphrasing here: "How can David, speaking by the Spirit, call the Messiah his Lord if he is also his son? Can the same Messiah be both the Father of David and Son of David at the same time?"

Now again, time for some technical language that carries great importance for getting inside the text at this crucial point:

In Psalm 110, a faithful translation of the Hebrew of the first clause is "Yahweh said to my Lord."

The Hebrew distinguishes between "Yahweh" as God the Father, on the one hand, and the "Lord" of David, on the other. In the Septuagint (LXX), which the Greek of Matthew 22:44 also quotes, it is *kurios to kurio*, or literally, "Lord to my Lord." Since the Jews had given up on the pronunciation of *Yahweh's* name between the time of Malachi and John the Baptist, they substituted for it the Hebrew *adonai*, which means "Lord," and which the Greek *kurios* also means.

Thus, from our modern perspective, we can miss the subtlety in this regard that the Pharisees know when Jesus quoted Psalm 110 – the generic "Lord to my Lord" being literally "Yahweh to my Lord." Or we can grasp it as "God the Father to God the Son" as it theologically unfolds. If we were not already apprised of Jesus' subtlety in his quote of Psalm 8, with the unspoken designation of the religious elitists as the enemies of the Messiah, we would also miss the force of Jesus' use of Psalm 110. The subtlety of the incarnational essence is at play – God in human form.

Jesus chooses the beginning of a text where Yahweh is speaking to the Messiah, a point not in dispute with the Pharisees. As Yahweh continues to speak to the Messiah in the subsequent verses, he says he will place the enemies of the Messiah under the Messiah's feet. Here is the first time in the text Jesus actually mentions the word "enemy." He now makes explicit the words from Psalm 8 that his enemies first acknowledged in their minds – they are the self-chosen enemies of the Messiah.

With the quote of Psalm 110, Jesus declares publicly that he has won the debate. His enemies are silenced – they are now under his feet. In fact, the whole debate is bookended by the two references to enemies – Psalm 8 at the beginning, internalized by the chief priests, and now, Psalm 110 as quoted by Jesus, the finale.

Also, when Jesus concludes with the question on how the Messiah can be both the Father of David and Son of David at the same time, he hints at the Trinitarian essence that the Pharisees would not, could not grasp, one that Jesus introduces in his quote from Psalm 8. Namely, the God whose strength is greater than the universe is the same God whose strength is manifest in childlikeness. Only a triune God can accomplish this – the God who at the same time governs the universe, while being incarnate as a human being through the Son, and as his Spirit erupts through the praise of the children.

The Messiah is both Lord of David and his Son at the same time. The Pharisees, because of their lust for worldly power, boxed God into their limited perspective and cannot perceive the reality of Yahweh Elohim as greater than space, time and number. Thus, they make him no greater than a pagan deity, as much as they would deny such an attitude. They can grasp neither the deity of the Messiah, nor the nature of salvation.

Matthew 21-22 is a literary unit that covers the debate Jesus has with his enemies. Here, at the end of it, Jesus brings the debate back to its point of origin, clears the detours, and there he stands, there the religious elitists stand, and there the delighted crowds stand. A moment of silence.

The enemies of Jesus, face to face, have already silenced themselves after posing Jesus four secondary questions. Thus, Jesus brings it back to the original question they had sought to avoid all along – the Son of David. Having done so, no one dares challenge him anymore, and now Jesus is free to continue his journey to the cross.

Chapter Eleven

Judgment and the Authority to Die

With the debate won and the enemies of Jesus muted by their own willpower, Jesus then has the freedom to pronounce judgment – to remove the influence of the religious elitists in their pollution of the people. Their static interference has been stilled. In Matthew 23, Jesus turns to the crowds and instructs the people to honor the position of the Pharisees, but not to do what they do, "for they do not practice what they preach" (v. 3). In contrast, Jesus preaches what he first practices, and his elitist opponents can find no fault in him. He calls his disciples to the opposite of self-aggrandizing elitism. Thus Jesus instructs the people as he has already taught his disciples: "The greatest among you will be your servant. For whoever exalts himself will be humbled, and whoever humbles himself will be exalted" (23:11-12).

Jesus then turns to the Pharisees and teachers of the law, his silenced enemies, in front of the crowds and delivers the "seven woes." Here we can sum it up in a paraphrase for the first portion: "Woe to you hypocrites who shut the kingdom of heaven in men's faces – you yourselves will not enter it! Woe to you hypocrites who labor to win a convert, only to make him twice as much a son of hell as you are! Woe to you blind guides who make foolish oaths and an idol out of the temple! Woe to you hypocrites who tithe but neglect justice, mercy and faithfulness – who strain at a gnat and swallow a camel! Woe to you hypocrites who cleanse the outside of the cup and dish, but inwardly are full of greed and self-indulgence! Woe to you hypocrites who look outwardly beautiful like a whitewashed tomb, but inside are full of dead men's bones and all uncleanness! Woe to you hypocrites who build tombs to honor slain prophets, whom you yourselves would have also slain!"

> "You snakes! You brood of vipers! How will you escape being condemned to hell? Therefore I am sending you prophets and wise men and teachers. Some of them you will kill and crucify; others you will flog in your synagogues and pursue from town to town. And so upon you will come all the righteous blood that has been shed on earth, from the blood of righteous Abel to the blood of Zechariah son of Berekiah, whom you murdered between the

temple and the altar. I tell you the truth, all this will come upon this generation.

> "O Jerusalem, Jerusalem, you who kill the prophets and stone those sent to you, how often I have longed to gather your children together, as a hen gathers her chicks under her wings, but you were not willing. Look, your house is left to you desolate. For I tell you, you will not see me again until you say, 'Blessed is he who comes in the name of the Lord' " (23:33-39).

Jesus uses the language of hell more than anyone in the Bible – and overwhelmingly directs it at people who hate mercy, here to the "sons of hell," or as in John 8:44, to his Pharisaical enemies as children of the devil. The Greek term for "hell" is *gehenna*, a transliteration from the Hebrew *ge'hinnom*, a shortened form for the Valley of Ben Hinnom. This valley, outside Jerusalem, is where the trash dump continually burns, and where in the waning days before the Babylonian destruction of the city 600 years earlier, the Jews descended into the practice of child sacrifice (see Jeremiah 19).

Thus, this metaphor defines what "hell" means for the Jewish listeners, and more powerfully yet for the Pharisees and teachers of the law who despise the praise of the children. The silenced enemies of Jesus are called by him "sons of hell," the most damning language in the Bible.

Then here, at the end of this delivered judgment, Jesus quotes Psalm 118:26, "Blessed is he who comes in the name of the Lord." He has come full circle from when he quoted it to the Pharisees who warned him not to come into Jerusalem (Luke 13:34-35), and from when people shouted it when he entered the city (Matthew 21:9).

These words are powerfully central to the Hebrew people and Messianic expectations. They are also said at Passover, and here Jesus is giving his last words to his enemies, and their supporters, in public, just before leaving the temple (24:1). He is saying, at least in part, that they will not see him again until they cite these very words at Passover. Or, in other words, he is indicating a prophetic nuance concerning himself as the Passover Lamb.

They will cite these words as part of the Passover ceremony, yet while also witnessing their very fulfillment.

The enemies of Jesus are silent as he delivers these words, and afterward as he leaves the public assembly and instructs his disciples on the signs that will precede the destruction of Jerusalem, and as well, for the end of the age. He instructs his disciples not to fall prey to the same Pharisaical idolatries.

And yet, even in the force of Jesus' pronouncement of judgment against his enemies, he laments for them. He cries out in agony, saying how he has always longed, and still even longs to gather them in his love, if only they were willing. Indeed, on the very cross they planned for him, he cries out, "Father, forgive them, for they do not know what they are doing" (Luke 23:34). But alas, they have refused the power of informed choice, even in seeing all the Messianic prophecies fulfilled. Jesus loves them enough to let them choose hell, they who hate mercy, and in his love he opposes their attempts to lead others to hell.

With his enemies silenced in public, they then reveal their true nature and slip into the ethics of the darkness, outside accountability to the people: "Then the chief priests and the elders of the people assembled in the palace of the high priest, whose name was Caiaphas, and they plotted to arrest Jesus in some sly way and kill him. 'But not during the Feast,' they said, 'or there may be a riot among the people' " (Matthew 26:3-5).

Judas is bought off to betray Jesus. As the betrayal takes place, and as Jesus refuses twelve legions of angels (some 72,000) to fight off the mob that has come to arrest him, he says: "Am I leading a rebellion, that you have come out with swords and clubs to capture me? Every day I sat in the temple courts teaching, and you did not arrest me. But this has all taken place that the writings of the prophets might be fulfilled" (26:55-56). Luke adds further words by Jesus here, "But this is your hour – when darkness reigns" (Luke 22:53).

Once the religious elitists cannot prevail on a level playing field, in the court of public opinion, they resort to the darkness of an illegal arrest and kangaroo trial late Thursday night and into early Friday morning of Passover.

136

They stack the deck and only invited other members of the Sanhedrin who also oppose Jesus.

In the illegal trial against Jesus, he is led before the high priest, Caiaphas. The chief priests and Sanhedrin seek evidence against Jesus to have him put to death as a blasphemer. They failed in the temple courts, and even with many false witnesses in the kangaroo court, they still fail. As Jesus said earlier concerning his life – "No one takes it from me, but I lay it down of my own accord. I have authority to lay it down and authority to take it up again" (John 10.18). He is in complete control of the level playing field, his death, his resurrection, and timetable.

Finally they find two men who claim that Jesus has said he would destroy and rebuild the temple in three days. In John 2:18-22, Jesus spoke these words in reference to the temple of his own body, but the Jewish elitists mistake him (deliberately in the final analysis) to mean Herod's temple, in their idolatry of it. So Caiaphas asks him if this is true. Jesus remains silent, for he has already answered all this in public. When Caiaphas charges him under oath to God to say if he were "the Christ, the Son of God" (Matthew 26:63), aka the Son of David, Jesus answers yes.

But living under Roman occupation, the Sanhedrin cannot put Jesus to death. They need the political authority of Pilate, the Roman governor, to do so. Thus, they bring Jesus before Pilate, and Jesus answers affirmatively his simple political question about being "king of the Jews" (a direct challenge to King Herod the Tetrarch). But when Jesus gives no answer to the accusations of the chief priests and elders in Pilate's presence, the governor wonders with amazement. When Pilate learned that Jesus is a Galilean (and thus outside his jurisdiction), he seeks to pass off the matter to King Herod, who is in Jerusalem at the time. Herod wants to see Jesus perform a miracle like a stage magician.

Herod, like the religious elitists, wanted Jesus dead from the outset, as we have already noted. So Jesus gives him no answer as well. All that is needful to say had been said in public already. Jesus does not allow himself to be pulled off his timetable or be deterred from his mission of deliverance and healing. Jesus has already judged Herod as a sneaky fox about the hen house, seeking only to devour.

So Herod sends Jesus back to Pilate, who is aware of the ulterior motivation of the religious elitists, and seeing no political threat to Jesus' claim as king of the Jews, he proposes to release him. But the Pharisees stir up a mob to cry for the release of Barabbas the murderer instead. Pilate's wife has a dream that day warning him not to "have anything to do with that innocent man" (Matthew 27:19), and sends word to her husband at that very moment. Instead, Pilate seeks a politically expedient way out. He declares there was "no basis" for a charge against Jesus. So Pilate washes his hands of the matter and turns Jesus over to the Sanhedrin's desire to put him to death, and they, with the mob they have assembled, cry, "Let his blood be on us and our children!" (Matthew 27:25).

Jesus takes the power of having silenced his enemies in public, and now in the restricted presence of the Sanhedrin's illegal meeting, he embraces the power to be silent before his accusers. He does so as the sacrificial lamb for Passover and Yom Kippur is mute before its shearers (Isaiah 53:7). He identifies his crucifiers as the religious elitists in particular – as the "shearers" of the Lamb of God for the final sacrifice. Indeed, as the atonement lamb is to be marched into the Court of the Gentiles to be examined under the Mosaic Law by the chief priests on Yom Kippur, to be sure it is without blemish; so too Jesus has already marched into the Court of the Gentiles and was examined by the chief priests in the debate, and they could find no fault in him.

Thus, his priestly enemies, et al., unwittingly confirm Jesus as the Lamb of God. As the whole debate unfolded, and afterward, the religious elitists must have had a gnawing and growing unease in their souls that by seeking to oppose Jesus as the Messiah, they were at the same time fulfilling the Messianic prophecies. Jesus has the authority to die, an authority they cannot, will not, understand, not being willing to repent of their sins. God sovereignly knows they were going to oppose and kill Jesus, though they knew the prophecies that made it clear. Yet they still freely chose to do so.

The Herodians and Herod play a secondary and utilitarian role in this temple and state conflict. The religious elitists are the ones who call the blood down upon their heads, and upon their children as self-chosen heirs of those who killed all the righteous saints, from Abel to Zechariah. And they also secured the hired mob to do the same.

It is hypocrites in religious dress who are the greatest threat to the Gospel, not politicians per se. Only because Jesus was able to silence these foes and avengers in public, with ethics that were above reproach, was he able to die for our sins as the blameless Lamb of God.

Chapter Twelve

Paradigm for Church and State

Jesus, in the face of his enemies, during Passover week, provides the true and complete paradigm for understanding church and state issues across the ages. Indeed, the means by which he purchases our salvation is that of the level playing field.

In the process, his character is revealed, and so too the character of all who witnessed him – those who believed in him, and those who plotted against him.

The biblical means to deal with hostility and censorship of the Gospel in the public arena is not in returning the same, but in offering the level playing field, where truth is uniquely afforded the opportunity to rise to the top. It is to give to those who would take from us, love those who hate us, and bless those who curse us. Light puts flight to darkness every time. Therefore, we must first live in the light.

In our study of the earthly and eternal political conflict during Passover week:

We see Jesus, the Son of David, using the Messianic praises of the people to enter the city and the temple area – the intersection of state and church. We see how worship defines the starting point for the engagement.

We see Jesus coming to challenge the idolatry of the temple, where true religion has been prostituted to prop up tyrannical political power.

We see Jesus coming to challenge a puppet tyrannical king, by his identity as the Suffering Servant in his first coming, and by the prophetic authority of the King of kings and Lord of lords in his Second Coming. His agenda is eternal, not temporal, but it shakes the temporal as nothing else can. His first act in the temple area is to cleanse it of economic evil, that which masquerades as a service to the Jewish pilgrims. After pronouncing judgment on this evil, healing power and mercy flows for the needy.

We see Jesus, both shrewd and innocent, as he fulfills the Messianic prophecies in the presence of his enemies. Part of his shrewdness is the strength of childlikeness in the face of human ego and pretense.

We see Jesus, not accusing his enemies, as he wishes for them redemption – rather, they accuse themselves, even reciting to themselves the clause in the Psalm 8 that reveals them to be the self-chosen enemies of the Messiah.

We see Jesus invite his enemies to a level playing field of open debate where they are free to rake him over the coals with their toughest questions, with no restrictions on their power to filibuster. In their questions, they immediately move away from the central issue of the Son of David, where they have already been silenced, and pose *four secondary questions*.

We see Jesus affirming the freedom of his enemies to pursue the secondary questions as intrinsic to a level playing field.

Their first question challenges his authority and credentials, and he responds with the power of the level playing field   posing them a question that aims back at the primary question they are avoiding. When, in seeking to give answer, they will not admit the truth, they cannot market a lie, so they pretend to be ignorant, the "I don't know" posture, the weakest form of moral argument in history.

We see Jesus then give them opportunity to see who they really are in a set of parables, but they refuse to see and understand. *They silenced themselves the first time.*

Their second question is a planned trap concerning church and state. But their own internal divisions are plain to see, being composed of erstwhile enemies in conspiracy, as they ineptly seek to use flattery to trap Jesus.

We see Jesus, in response, call them what they are – hypocrites – but he still gives them the level playing field to continue the debate.

We see Jesus, again in response, asking to see the evidence (i.e. the denarius coin). Indeed, the facts of the case, a true definition of terms, always lead to the truth. The real conflict is brought into the open – a false son of god versus the true Son of God, a false messiah versus the true Messiah. *They silenced themselves the second time.*

Their third question is one of theological nitpicking, pretending to be serious when they are not, and again revealing their internal divisions.

We see Jesus giving answer with his command of the Scriptures, their ignorance of the same, and thus turning their question on its head. *They silenced themselves the third time.*

Their fourth question is one of theological grandstanding concerning the greatest commandment of all.

We see Jesus answer it easily, *and they stood there with nothing more to say – silenced for the fourth time.*

We see Jesus, having answered the four secondary questions, now returning the debate to square one – whose son is the Christ? They avoided it before, but now that their secondary questions have fallen flat, they are self-cornered into answering correctly – the Son of David, but without wanting to acknowledge Jesus as the Son.

His enemies now have to grapple with the question – the Son of David – they have sought to avoid all along. They cannot, would not, address it the first time, and now, having been self-silenced following their four diversions, they have nowhere to turn but honesty or self-condemnation. Happily, at least one teacher of the law chooses the former – the exception that proves the rule.

We see Jesus then pose a final question that reveals how they do not know the biblical reality of their answer, they do not grasp the nature of God the Father and God the Son, *and they dare not ask him any more questions.*

They silence themselves publicly – first in their initial non-answer to the quote of Psalm 8 relative to the Son of David, second with respect to their four secondary questions, and finally as Jesus returns the debate to the first and definitive question.

We see Jesus, having won the debate, with reference to a key Messianic prophecy, now being free to judge his enemies in public, though he deeply laments their chosen state.

We see Jesus, now free to proceed to the cross as the blameless Lamb of God, having submitted to the toughest questions of his sworn enemies in public debate, and thus having purchased the authority to die and rise again on behalf of those who believe in him.

And throughout the whole debate, the poor and needy – those seeking mercy – rejoice.

In earthly terms, it is hypocritical religious elitists who drove the political decision to crucify Jesus.

As believers meditate on the storyline and text of Jesus in the face of his enemies, we are empowered to become effective as salt and light in the political world. We see an ethic and pattern that transcends history, one that is universally applicable in grasping the biblical nature of church and state. What are the possibilities?

1. We are able to worship freely in the public arena, while at the same time addressing political concerns, in concert with the same religious liberty honored for all people equally.

2. We are free to proclaim Jesus as the Son of David, King of kings and Lord of lords; in concert with the same religious liberty honored for all people equally to proclaim their allegiances.

3. We are free to live holy lives as temples of the Holy Spirit, serving the cleansing of the church from hypocrisy and idolatry.

4. We are free to embrace the innocence and shrewdness of the strength of childlikeness.

5. We are free to advance the power of the level playing field – where by definition truth rises to the top, and the pretension of ignorance is overcome by a focus on true definition of terms.

6. We are free to use our earthly citizenship to advance the coming kingdom of God, being fearless in speaking truth to power – even in the face of lethal opposition.

7. We are free to remove static interference to the Gospel, remove false barriers, and thus empower the grasp of justice and mercy as a taste of the power of the age to come.

This is only possible by the grace of God the Father, in the name of Jesus and through the power of the Holy Spirit.

Also, on top of Jesus being the Son of David, if we were to examine each of the four angles that the enemies of Jesus took – challenging his authority and credentials, posing the church and state conflict, and harping on theological nitpicking and theological grandstanding – we would discover that there is nothing new under the sun.

♦ ♦ ♦

Therefore, in the face of political evil, we need to grasp who Jesus is.

If a modest core of biblically rooted believers in our midst were to run for political office, success would come to pass – as rooted in a rigorous embrace of the level playing field, where skeptics are genuinely heard and given freedom to pose their toughest questions.

If the church were to become truly biblical, nations will shake, tyrants will come crashing down in the implosion of their own devices, and people of good will everywhere will rejoice.